PASTORAL LEADERSHIP

PASTORAL LEADERSHIP

A Handbook of Resources for Effective
Congregational Leadership

ROBERT D. DALE

Abingdon Press
Nashville

PASTORAL LEADERSHIP

Copyright © 1986 by Abingdon Press

Fourth Printing 1990

Third Printing 1989

This book is printed on acid-free paper.

Library of Congress Cataloging-in-Publication Data

DALE, ROBERT D.
  Pastoral leadership.
  Includes indexes.
  1. Pastoral theology. 2. Christian leadership. I. Title.
  BV4011.D35   1986   253   85-22832
     ISBN 0-687-30349-4
     (pbk.: alk. paper)

Illustrations are from: Robert D. Dale, *Ministers as Leaders* (Nashville:
Broadman Press, 1984), pp. 19, 56, 59, 117, and *To Dream Again* (Nashville:
Broadman Press, 1981), p. 17; Ernest Mosley, *Called to Joy* (Nashville:
Convention Press, 1973), pp. 25-26; Bob R. Taylor, *The Work of the Minister
of Youth* (Nashville: Convention Press, 1982), p. 105. All rights reserved.
Used by permission.

Scripture quotations unless otherwise noted are from the Revised
Standard Common Bible, copyright © 1973 by the Division of Christian
Education of the National Council of Churches in the U.S.A. and are used
by permission. All rights reserved.

MANUFACTURED IN THE UNITED STATES OF AMERICA

A C K N O W L E D G M E N T S

I SEE LOTS of faces in this book's pages. Slightly more than a quarter century of ministry involvement underlies this book, half of that time in local church leadership and half of it in teaching others to lead. I owe thanks to lots of people for these twenty-six years of experience. I've learned from several strong leaders, and I've also failed often enough to learn from my own weaknesses. A composite of experiences as pastor, staff minister, denominational consultant, and seminary professor reminds me that thank you to many persons is appropriate.

You will note from the bibliographies scattered throughout the book that I've also learned from many writers and researchers on leadership topics. I've limited the reading lists to books only for reasons of space.

One special word of appreciation is due to Mary Lou Stephens and Mary Ida Buzhardt for their thoughtful and productive work in preparing the manuscript for Abingdon's able editorial staff. Thanks are also due to Peggy Haymes, Jim Manchester, and Doug Frazier for freeing me from some responsibilities.

CONTENTS

DEAR READER:

When I open a book, I want to know two things immediately. First, what's this book about? Second, how can I get the most from it the fastest? Let me help you read this book by telling you what it's about and how to read it.

This book is about pastoral leadership in a congregational setting. Pastoral leadership is defined, described, and applied in the pages that follow.

You can read this book in either of two ways.

● One, you can sit down and read it from cover to cover, each page and chapter in the order of printing. That's a nice way to absorb a book. But, frankly, most of us don't have the time to read books that way often. (Most books aren't written beginning at the title page and composing straight through to the final page either.)
● Or, you can read it as a problem-solver. When some leadership challenge occurs, you can scan the table of contents or one of the indices, find where your concern is treated, and dip into the book to get what you need. Then, you can refer to the book again the next time you're stumped by some leadership situation.

If you use this handbook as a problem-solving tool, here's a "map" for overviewing what's between these covers.

- What's pastoral leadership? How does it fit congregations? (See chapter 1.)
- What are some theological, biblical, and philosophical bases for understanding pastoral leadership? (See chapters 1, 2, and 5.)
- What are some leader style options for ministers? (See chapters 3 and 4.)
- What are some essential leader skills? (See the "laboratory" in chapters 6–14.)
- What are some personal issues leaders in ministry commonly face? (See chapters 15–18.)

The following chapters are linked but free-standing. That is, all the chapters taken together are intended to trace the theme of congregational leadership consistently and coherently. However, each chapter is also designed to be read as a separate essay, if you have the time, need, or interest to read only a single chapter.

Each chapter ends with an overview and a short series of review questions to provide a brief recap of the chapter's contents. Further, a selected bibliography is matched with each topic to enable you to dig more deeply into themes of special interest to you.

Thanks for your interest in providing quality leadership in your congregation! Happy reading. And, more importantly, happy leading!

Bob Dale
Wake Forest, North Carolina

I.
Seeing Leadership in Congregational Context: Practical and Theological Perspectives

— 1 —

FOUNDATIONS FOR
A MINISTRY OF
LEADERSHIP

AN UNDISTINGUISHED MINISTER received a fancy letter in the mail. From the expensive looking envelope he took a sheet of parchment-like stationery. To his utter surprise, the letter invited him to become the president of one of his denomination's most prestigious institutions. "Why," he wondered, "have they turned to me?" The minister didn't consider himself famous or worthy of such lofty recognition. Musing on his own question to himself, the minister absent-mindedly turned the envelope over and over in his hands. Suddenly his eyes spied a line that brought a smile to his lips and answered his personal inquiry. The envelope was addressed to "Boxholder"!

Wryly, this story reminds us of a crucial fact: we live in a strange time for leadership. We beg for leaders to lead. Then, either we demand they act God-like in judgment and character or we insist they do nothing without our advance knowledge and complete support. No wonder experts write about why leaders can't lead.[1]

Who Are Leaders?
What Do They Do in Congregations?

Pastors must be congregational leaders. Fortunately, we aren't the only leaders in our churches. But we must provide leadership in the congregation. It goes with the territory.

Generally defined, leadership is an action-oriented, interpersonal influencing process.[2] In essence, leadership involves vision and initiative. More comprehensively, pastoral leaders see visions of ministry, communicate our dreams clearly, gain consensus and commitment to common objectives, take initiative by setting the pace in ministry actions, and multiply our influence by transforming followers into new leaders. Pastoral leaders differ from church managers. Church managers conserve and concentrate on doing things right; pastoral leaders create and focus on doing the right things.

How Leaders Act

Leadership doesn't occur in theory. Leaders act out of real values and in concrete situations. How, then, do pastoral leaders behave in congregational settings?

Pastoral Leaders Are Visionaries

A dream of ministry provides a launching pad for leading congregations. Pastoral leaders are highly conscious of what we want out of life and in ministry. An "I have a dream" vision frequently stimulates a "yes, me too" response. Napoléon Bonaparte recognized the visionary element of leadership. He asserted that "a leader is a dealer in hope." He was correct. Effective leaders are adept at living out the sentiment of George Bernard Shaw: "You see things; and you say, 'Why?' But I dream of things that never were; and I say, 'Why not?' "

Pastoral Leaders Articulate Our Dreams Imaginatively

Some historians now say the genius of Franklin Roosevelt's leadership was his ability to project American idealism. Whether in words (like Jesus' parables) or in symbolic deeds (like Jesus' enacted parables), leaders have a knack for finding the right metaphor for expressing our vision of ministry. To illustrate, one leader installed an automotive seat belt on his desk chair to communicate to his followers that the organization was taking off.

Pastoral Leaders Develop Psychological Ownership of the Dream in Our Followers

Good leaders give our followers "a piece of the action." Because people support what they help create, pastoral leaders build consensus, commitment, and momentum for implementing projects by involving the members of the congregation early and often in dreaming and planning.

Pastoral Leaders Take the Risks of Initiative

Faith requires risk taking. The book of Hebrews describes faith as "the assurance of things hoped for, the conviction of things not seen" (Heb. 11:1). Wags have claimed that some leaders look for a parade and then proceed to get in front of it. In contrast, real leaders go out ahead to show the way.[3] We step out.

Pastoral Leaders Don't Wait for "Perfect" Circumstances Before Acting

Initiative requires acting even (or especially) when the leadership situation is ambiguous. In the words of singer and poet Harry Chapin, "When in doubt, do something." Leaders in the field of rehabilitative medicine apply one principle consistently: action offsets anxiety. These specialists know that our fears freeze us up. But acting unsticks us and puts us in charge of our life situations. Importantly, the possibility of failure doesn't cow effective leaders. We demonstrate the "Wallenda effect." Like Karl Wallenda, the famed tightrope walker, effective leaders focus all our energies on the tightrope. The risk of falling and failing doesn't paralyze effective leaders. If we slip, we learn from our mistakes and move again.

Pastoral Leaders Transform Our Followers into Leaders[4]

Secure leaders know our worth to the kingdom of God. Consequently, we believe in the potential, motives, and skills of our followers. Seeing the possibilities of ministry to the kingdom of God in others encourages them to grow. These followers are empowered. New growth, power, and confidence open the doors to transformation, and tomorrow's leadership emerges from yesterday's followers.

Pastoral Leaders Are Bifocal

Effective leaders balance relationships and results, climate and content, unchanging convictions and varying circumstances for ministry. We realize that leadership is a rich and diverse opportunity. Sensitive leaders avoid tunnel vision by maintaining a bifocal perspective on our stewardship of ministry occasions.

Pastoral Leaders Know When and How to Follow

Leadership and followership aren't static relationships. Roles shift back and forth between leading and following in congregations. In different circumstances or on different issues, dreamers become doers or activists fill a visionary function. The relationship between leaders and followers remains constantly fluid, dynamic, and vital in congregational settings.

Pastoral Leaders Aren't All Pastors

Pastoral leadership is viewed broadly. That is, pastoral leaders provide a service to their congregations instead of filling a role. Therefore, staff ministers (other than pastors) and lay members serve their congregations in shepherding initiatives.

Pastoral Leaders Are Congregationalists

Effective leaders take a generalist, corporate, system-wide view of the congregation at large. The health and direction of the overall enterprise is our touchstone. Pastors and other congregational leaders don't have the luxury of narrowing our focus to specialty skills or one-issue perspectives.

Fitting Leadership into the Larger Picture

Each of us has a picture in our heads about how the world works. This frame of reference gives us "a track to run on" in life and in work. Our mental picture of reality, held consciously or unconsciously, shapes how we act and react. We have a guiding perspective for leadership's place in our ministries too.

What's your model for ministry, including leadership? One helpful design for pastoral ministries views ministry functionally. That is, ministry can be cast in a framework of what must be done in Christ's name. Broadly described, Christian ministry calls on us to (1) proclaim the gospel to believers and unbelievers by means of preaching and worship as well as evangelism and nurture, (2) care for the church's members and other persons in the community through pastoral counseling and visitation as well as family ministries and grief support, and (3) lead the church in the achievement of its mission.[5] Proclaim, care, and lead. That's the functional baseline for ministry.

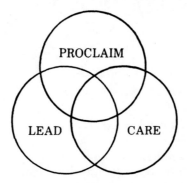

Illustration 1. Ministry Functions Model

This model may be misapplied several ways. (1) Some pastors may see ourselves as specialists in one of these areas to the exclusion of the other functions. Balance in ministry suffers under this circumstance.

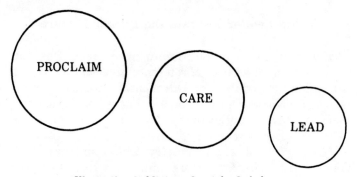

Illustration 2. Ministry Specialty Imbalance

(2) Other church leaders balance proclamation, caring, and leading. However, these ministers keep each function separate from the others. While balanced, we lose the opportunity to blend and integrate our ministry efforts.

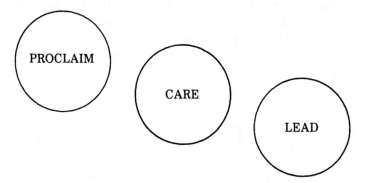

Illustration 3. Separate-but-Equal Misapplication

(3) Another common misapplication in some congregations involves assigning some functions to clergy-type ministers and others to laity-type ministers. In many

cases, preaching and evangelism and counseling are made the responsibility and territory of the clergyperson and administration the arena of laypersons. In this circumstance no one retains a corporate or overall perspective on the health and mission of the congregation. Then, both leaders and congregation suffer.

| Clergy Leader's
Ministry Arenas | | Lay Leader's
Ministry Arena |

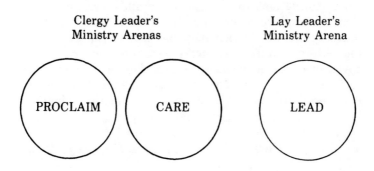

Illustration 4. Clergy-Laity Misapplication

Ideally, a balanced, unified, and team-oriented application of this three-function model provides rich ministry in and beyond the congregation. In this mental picture proclaiming, caring, and leading are lived out in equal fashion. Additionally, this model consolidates all three functions into an overlapping approach that allows and encourages blending ministry responsibilities together. By deliberately *working in the overlap areas,* pastoral leaders can lead and proclaim when we preach on stewardship or when we orient new members to the congregation's vision. This perspective helps us work smarter rather than just harder. Finally, team ministry is fostered by the ministerial staff of the congregation, clergy and lay, joining in service to assure that the work of the church is complete and integrated.

Congregations as Leadership Arenas

Congregations are the leadership arenas this book focuses on. These local communities of faith are challenging settings for pastoral leadership. The reasons for the challenges vary. (1) Congregations are volunteer organizations. As such, congregations are among the most sophisticated organizations we humans design. Unfortunately, we know more about business and industrial organizations than about service and nonprofit ones. (2) Volunteers join and participate for a range of motives. Their motivations are more altruistic and service-oriented than the employees most of us have met in the commercial marketplace. (3) Participative methods fit congregations and other volunteer agencies best. Bossing and other power-oriented supervisory approaches are common in secular management circles. Only dependent volunteer members, however, are comfortable with nonparticipative leader styles in congregational settings.

Looking at Personal Leadership in Congregations

Proclaiming, caring, and leading—how do these ministry functions mesh in a congregational setting? Basically, what's important is that all three broad functions are lived out in balance by a congregation's members. Not

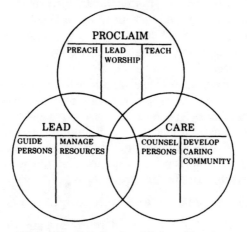

Illustration 5. Balancing Ministry Functions

everyone is equally gifted or involved in each of the three areas. But all three ministry functions need to be provided within and beyond the congregation.

Since this book spotlights leadership, let's examine the relationship between these three ministry functions from the perspective of pastoral leadership. Consider pastoral leadership historically, socially, and congregationally.

Historically, a shift is occurring in the application of pastoral skills to congregational life. Traditionally, proclamation skills—preaching, teaching, leading worship, and evangelizing—have been stressed in mainstream Protestant groups. In some denominational circles, proclamation was the central, almost exclusive, emphasis in congregations until about the middle of this present century. Then, after World War II a new, professionalized ministry thrust gained momentum, growing out of the clinical pastoral education movement. The caring skills of pastoral counseling, clinical chaplaincy in hospital settings, grief intervention, and ministry to family systems expanded the congregational leader's array of tools. A third force is now emerging in pastoral skills. Pastoral leadership is building on the motivation and communication skills of proclaiming and the human relations skills of counseling. Additionally, leadership studies in ministry draw from the significant learnings of industrial psychology, business administration, and organizational research. Seminaries are updating our old church administration courses and are developing practical theology courses on leadership, pastoral management, congregational health, and organizational development.

From the social perspective of the community of faith, proclaiming usually is practiced one-to-many. Caring is often one-to-one or one-to-a-few. Pastoral leadership involves working in a challenging blending of public and private settings. Participative processes are fundamental to effective pastoral leadership.

Congregationally, leadership can be used as a lens through which we can examine proclaiming, caring, and managing. Preaching, for instance, provides a prime opportunity for leaders. In this role, we can articulate the congregation's vision, model the congregation's atmosphere and mood, and demonstrate our trustworthiness and credibility. Or, to illustrate from the angle of caring, leadership is shown concretely in the development of support structures and problem-solving procedures. Finally, leaders as administrators model effective self-management and a trust for congregational processes and policies.

The Fabric and Threads of Leadership

An overall view of leadership creates a piece of whole cloth, a fabric, for leading. Within the larger fabric, however, are the individual threads which are woven together to make up our leadership. Our attitudes about leadership arise from a variety of threads or sources.[6]

Briefly, let's identify some of the more crucial strands of our viewpoints on exercising leadership. One thread in our leadership pattern is how we saw our parents and other authority figures take initiative and solve problems. Another strand in our leadership approach is the way we understood the vision of our heroes and heroines, our models and mentors. An additional leadership thread involves how we view American character and regional or cultural values. Still another fiber in our leadership fabric is our understanding of biblical leaders and our denominational traditions of leadership. All these threads combine into the unique texture of our perspective on leadership. Most of these factors in our leadership fabrics are explored later in this book.

Overview: Pastoral Leadership Foundations

Pastoral leadership is an action-oriented, interpersonal influencing process practiced in a congregational setting. While pastoral leaders basically demonstrate vision and initiative, we behave in diverse ways to provide a pace-setting role for our congregations. Further, pastoral leaders are savvy about volunteers and service organizations.

Review Questions

1. What is leadership?
2. How do pastoral leaders behave?
3. How can an integrated model of pastoral leadership be depicted?

Notes

1. Warren Bennis, *The Unconscious Conspiracy: Why Leaders Can't Lead* (New York: AMACOM, 1976).
2. James J. Cribbin, *Leadership: Strategies for Organizational Effectiveness* (New York: AMACOM, 1981), p. v.
3. Robert K. Greenleaf, *Servant Leadership* (Ramsey, N.J.: Paulist Press, 1977), p. 15.
4. James MacGregor Burns, *Leadership* (New York: Harper & Row, 1978), p. 20.
5. This model is drawn from Ernest E. Mosley's, *Called to Joy: Design for Pastoral Ministries* (Nashville: Convention Press, 1973), pp. 12-28. All rights reserved. Used by permission.
6. Robert D. Dale, *Ministers as Leaders* (Nashville: Broadman Press, 198), pp. 28-51.

Selected Bibliography on Pastoral Leadership

The bibliographies appearing later in this book are much leaner than this one. This reading list includes a range of leadership resources to help pastoral leaders understand our craft practically and theologically as well as the broader field of leadership.

Adams, Arthur Merrihew. *Effective Leadership for Today's Church.* Philadelphia: Westminster Press, 1978.

Barber, James David. *The Presidential Character: Predicting Performance in the White House.* Englewood Cliffs, N.J.: Prentice-Hall, 1977.

Bennis, Warren. *The Unconscious Conspiracy: Why Leaders Can't Lead.* New York: AMACOM, 1976.

Burns, James MacGregor. *Leadership.* New York: Harper & Row, 1978.

Cribbin, James J. *Leadership: Strategies for Organizational Effectiveness.* New York: AMACOM, 1981.

Dale, Robert D. *Ministers as Leaders.* Nashville: Broadman Press, 1984.

———. *Surviving Difficult Church Members.* Nashville: Abingdon Press, 1984.

———. *To Dream Again.* Nashville: Broadman Press, 1981.

Doohan, Helen. *Leadership in Paul.* Wilmington, Del.: Michael Glazier, 1984.

Engstrom, Ted W. *The Making of a Christian Leader.* Grand Rapids: Zondervan Corp., 1976.

Fiedler, Fred E., et al. *Improving Leadership Effectiveness: The Leader Match Concept.* New York: John Wiley & Sons, 1976.

Gordon, Thomas. *Leadership Effectiveness Training.* New York: Bantam Books, 1980.

Greenleaf, Robert K. *Servant Leadership.* Ramsey, N.J.: Paulist Press, 1977.

Hollander, Edwin P. *Leadership Dynamics: A Practical Guide to Effective Relationships.* New York: The Free Press, 1978.

Keating, Charles J. *The Leadership Book,* rev. ed. Ramsey, N.J.: Paulist Press, 1978.

Mosley, Ernest E., ed. *Leadership Profiles from Bible Personalities.* Nashville: Broadman Press, 1979.

Peters, Thomas J., and Waterman, Robert H., Jr. *In Search of Excellence: Lessons from America's Best-Run Companies.* New York: Harper & Row, 1982.

Richardson, William B., and Feldhusen, John F. *Leadership Education.* West LaFayette, Ind.: William Richardson Enterprises, 1984.

Sanders, J. Oswald. *Paul the Leader.* Colorado Springs, Co.: Navpress, 1984.

———. *Spiritual Leadership.* Chicago: Moody Press, 1967.

Schillebeeckx, Edward. *Ministry: Leadership in the Community of Jesus Christ.* New York: Crossroad, 1981.

Stogdill, Ralph M. *Handbook of Leadership: A Survey of Theory and Research.* New York: The Free Press, 1974.

CHAPTER

— 2 —

SERVANTHOOD:
THE PRIMARY BIBLICAL
IMAGE OF LEADERSHIP

THE BIBLE IS filled with rich models for pastoral leaders. Kings, priests, prophets and prophetesses, sages, Sanhedrin members, family and household authorities, the synagogue structure, the Pharisee and Essene communities, Greek democracy, the secular trade guilds, Roman rulers, pastors and elders, bishops, deacons, apostles, and missionaries provide possibilities for leadership perspectives.

Since so many biblical options are available to us, how do we make a selection from the alternatives? A basic beginning point for Christians is to examine the leader stance and style of Jesus. No single New Testament passage clearly specifies a leader approach. But, woven into the fabric of the biblical record is a pattern that appears to fit Jesus' life and work. That pattern is servanthood.

Each of the Synoptic Gospels makes a comparison between the secular rulers and the servanthood model (Matt. 20:20-28; Mark 10:35-44; Luke 22:24-27). The statement that the person who wishes to be greatest must become a servant appears at least seven times in the Gospels (Matt. 20:27-28 and 23:11; Mark 9:35 and 10:43-44; Luke 9:48 and 22:26-27; and John 13:14). These passages spotlight the servant alternative for Christian leaders. Let's use the servant perspective as a framework for surveying types of leaders in the Bible.

Servant Leaders in the Old Testament

Kings, judges, prophets and prophetesses, priests, and sages are mainstream examples of Old Testament leaders.[1] Each provided a different kind of service to Israel.

Kings: serving as God's representatives.—A variety of attitudes about the role of Israel's king is seen in the Old Testament. Unlike other Eastern dictators who stood apart from their subjects, Israel's king was subject to God's law the same as the people. The prophets, therefore, could and did rebuke the kings (1 Sam. 12 and 1 Kings 21). Ultimately, God was Israel's ruler. The kings, then, had leadership only as long as they functioned as God's vice-regents. These kings led Israel into the missionary responsibilities of a servant nation (Isa. 49, esp. vss. 5-6). They are pictured as shepherds who served God and the nation by providing care and protection (Ezek. 34; Isa. 44:28; Jer. 23:1-4).

Judges: serving as periodic rescuers of God's people.— The judges served Israel as temporary leaders who helped deliver local tribes from their destructive cycles of sin and idolatry. In early Hebrew history, there was tension in some Israelites' minds between the sophisticated festivals of Baalism and the simplicity of their desert religion. They fell into a pattern of idolatry (Judg. 6:25-26). A cycle of sin, oppression, deliverance, and faithfulness was repeated throughout the time of the judges (Judg. 2:11-19). These judges were local military heroes and heroines who provided temporary inspiration to deliver Israel from her self-destructiveness.

Priests, prophets, and prophetesses: serving the nation's religious needs.—The priests led the worship activities of Israel and specialized mainly in religious ceremonies. Their leadership was mostly behind the scenes and, therefore, provides minimal information on leader options

for modern ministers. Likewise, the prophets and prophetesses as leaders are difficult to translate into local church
settings. Their function later became more visible and
moved beyond religion to politics.

Sages: serving as godly tutors to royalty.—The sages of
the Old Testament were crucial, although not highly
visible, leaders. These educators/advisers served as mind-
molders for royalty and public leaders. After the Exile,
they rose in prominence and became equal in influence
with the priests and prophets who weren't as numerous by
that time. The sages valued their favored position near the
seats of power; their counsel, consequently, tended to be
practical and politically conservative. Their starting
point, however, was typically religious: "The fear of the
Lord is the beginning of knowledge; fools despise wisdom
and instruction" (Prov. 1:7).

Servant Leaders in the New Testament

Like the Old Testament, the New Testament offers a
variety of leader models. Some, like pastors and deacons,
served in local church settings. They preached and
witnessed to the life and work of Jesus, cared for the
congregation and community, and set the pace as the
congregation pursued its ministry goals. Others, like the
apostles, provided missionary leadership. Paul, Peter,
James, and Barnabas offer additional personal examples
of Christian leadership during the New Testament era.

The primary New Testament leader is obviously Jesus
Christ. From beginning to end, Jesus' ministry demonstrates servanthood. When Jesus declared his ministry, he
depicted himself as a servant. Read Luke 4:1-21 for a
description of Jesus' struggle about ministry style.

The Tempter suggested three alternative approaches to
leadership in Luke 4. (1) Jesus could have adopted the
"pleasure principle" as a basis for his ministry. Satisfying
legitimate and obvious physical needs of others and self is
one option for leaders. The Tempter advised, "Tell these

loaf-shaped desert stones to become bread; you deserve to eat after the soul struggle you've endured." This issue would appear again later in Jesus' ministry when the satisfied crowds wanted him to become their meat-and-potatoes Messiah (John 6:1-15, 25-27). But Jesus decided his ministry would not focus on providing personal pleasure.

(2) Jesus also had the option of using the "power principle" of leadership. The Tempter offered rulership over all the kingdoms of the earth. At that time, the popular Jewish expectation envisioned a warrior Messiah like David, a General Patton—like commander who would assure that Israel's traditional enemies finally got their just deserts. But when Jesus made his triumphal entry into Jerusalem, he rode a donkey rather than a war horse. Military force and political intrigue obviously weren't his preference either.

(3) Jesus had the "parade principle" recommended to him by the Tempter too. Jesus could have jumped from the Temple's high roof into angels' arms. Although he had miraculous power, Jesus also refused a magic ministry and the popular curiosity it would have aroused.

Jesus chose the "service principle" instead. Servanthood would become the leader approach for the kingdom of God. His leadership stance is defined in the Nazareth Manifesto. Note his own words:

> The Spirit of the Lord is upon me,
> because he has anointed me to preach good news to the poor.
> He has sent me to proclaim release to the captives
> and recovering of sight to the blind,
> to set at liberty those who are oppressed,
> to proclaim the acceptable year of the Lord. (Luke 4:18-19)

At the end of Jesus' ministry another outstanding example of servanthood is clearly visible. At the Last Supper, Jesus wrapped himself with a towel, took a basin of water, and proceeded to wash the disciples' feet (John 13:4-5). Jesus both launched and concluded his ministry as a servant.

Jesus as a Leader

Servanthood is a basic image of the person and work of Christ. For example, when the hymn fragment containing the loftiest Christology in the New Testament describes Jesus, what term does it use? Servant. Paul notes that in the incarnation Jesus "emptied himself, taking the form of a servant" (Phil. 2:7). The introduction to the Fourth Gospel shows the same contrast. The Word who had companioned with God and was God practiced downward mobility and pitched his tent in our midst. Servanthood is implied in the images of the Gospel: "And the Word became flesh and dwelt among us" (John 1:14).

Jesus himself couches leaders' actions in terms of servanthood in one of the premier passages on leadership in the New Testament. After his third direct attempt to prepare his disciples for his arrest, crucifixion, and resurrection, James and John pressed him to make them Vice-President and Secretary of State in the messianic regime. Jesus asked them if they could accept and endure the same hardships he must face. Their easy agreement and the anger of the ten other disciples prompted Jesus to state three principles.

First, the worldly view of success, greatness, and power isn't Jesus' definition. He asserted, "You know that those who are supposed to rule over the Gentiles lord it over them, and their great men exercise authority over them. But it shall not be so among you . . . " (Mark 10:42-43).

Second, service is the measure of Christian leadership. Jesus noted that ". . . . whoever would be great among you must be your servant, and whoever would be first among you must be slave of all" (Mark 10:43-44).

Third, servanthood for Christians is modeled on Jesus' own behaviors. He reminded them: "For the Son of man also came not to be served but to serve, and to give his life as a ransom for many" (Mark 10:45).

This passage illustrates that servanthood is a Christian stance for leadership. In fact, the entire Gospel of Mark can be approached as a case study on the servant stance for Christian leaders.[2]

Servanthood as a Leadership Stance: The Gospel of Mark, a Case Study

Christian Leaders Are Servants of People (Mark 1:1–4:34)

Mark's Gospel has a hurried, yet orderly, flavor about it. It spills over with fast-moving words like "straightway" and "immediately." Some interpreters have called Mark the "motion picture" Gospel and feel its bias toward active service is a reflection of Simon Peter's impetuous nature. Amid the rapidly paced events of Mark's Gospel, the saving acts of Jesus are revealed.

Mark presents the essence of Jesus' ministry in deeds. Mark's Gospel concentrates more on the works of Jesus, his miracles, than on the words of Jesus, his parables. To illustrate, Jesus' service to others is described in several incidents. Healing the paralytic in Mark 2:1-12 and healing the man's withered hand in Mark 3:1-6 show Jesus' care for persons in spite of the opposition these acts attracted. Interestingly, the demons recognized Jesus' identity and power first (Mark 1:24-26; 3:11).

Christian Leaders Are Servants of God (Mark 4:35–8:26)

Because Jesus was God's servant, he did mighty acts of mercy. He calmed the sea, his first nature miracle (Mark 4:35-41). The Creator serves and commands the creation. Jesus cast the demons out of a Gentile schizophrenic (Mark 5:1-20), and the Gadarene became the first missionary to the Gentiles. The implication? God loves all his people. God's servant also overcame chronic illness (Mark 5:25-34) and even death (Mark 5:35-43). Jesus healed the Syrophoenician woman's daughter (Mark 7:24-30) and fed four thousand (Mark 8:1-10). In these and a myriad of other startling acts, Jesus proved again and again his servanthood of a powerful God.

Christian Leaders Are
Servants with a Mission (Mark 8:27–10:52)

Peter's confession of Jesus as Messiah provides the hinge passage of Mark's Gospel (Mark 8:27-33). Jesus' servant role changes from section to section of Mark's Gospel. However, servanthood remains the constant attitude of the book.

The Cross event is a core anchor to orient the Christian life around. Jesus notes, "If any man would come after me, let him deny himself and take up his cross and follow me. For whoever would save his life will lose it; and whoever loses his life for my sake and the gospel's will save it" (Mark 8:34-35). When folks have something worth living and dying for, they have found fulfillment. They have a mission, a vision of life.

Typical of Mark's record, the mountain-top experiences and the valleys of frustration are linked together. The Transfiguration, one of the crucial identifying and affirming events in Jesus' life, is followed by a healing of an epileptic boy—a result denied to the nine disciples who had stayed in the valley. They hadn't availed themselves of the power of intercessory prayer (Mark 9:1-29).

Twice in this section of the Gospel account, Jesus points out that greatness comes from what we do for others. In his description of his impending Passion (Mark 9:30-32) and in his affirmation of servanthood and childlikeness (Mark 9:33-37) Jesus raises up a new standard of judgment. We are to evaluate ourselves and others on the basis of what we do, not what we say.

Mark closes this section with Jesus' pivotal teaching on greatness (Mark 10:32-52). True greatness doesn't result from earthly power—like Rome and its rule by sword. True greatness is service. The more you serve, the greater you become. To improve the point, Jesus referred again to his ultimate service, the Cross. Jesus had a messianic mission. In Jesus, the world saw the real Messiah and was surprised to realize that the Messiah would carry the towel and basin of a servant.

Christian Leaders Serve Prophetically (Mark 11–13)

As God's champion, Jesus showed the residents of Jerusalem and the visiting Passover pilgrims the attitude of God. The Triumphal Entry into Jerusalem demonstrated the Messiah as a servant. Jesus entered the city on a lowly beast of burden. Jesus conquers by humble service, not by force. This entrance to the chief city was an enacted parable, a prophetic demonstration.

Jesus warns us against a lack of productivity in the cursing of the fig tree (Mark 11:12-14, 20-26) and against the perversion of worship in the cleansing of the temple (Mark 11:15-19). In the "Little Apocalypse" of Mark 13, Jesus gives an additional warning statement about the future.

On his third day in Jerusalem, Jesus encountered the Jewish leaders—priests, scribes, elders, Pharisees, Herodians, and Sadducees. He answered their questions easily. For example, when asked which commandment is primary, Jesus gave us the Great Commandment (Mark 12:29-31). Loving God with all that we are and have is a tall order. To add that we are also to love our neighbors as we love ourselves makes a practical demand on our daily living patterns.

Jesus further spotlighted the widow who gave her entire income—two mites—to the temple treasury. She's credited with giving the largest gift of all—everything. Jesus illustrated that God isn't impressed with the value of material possessions. Gifts to God are calculated on their value to the person who offers them to God.

Christian Leaders Are Empowered by a God Who Suffered and Rose Again (Mark 14–16)

Mark rightly places the death and resurrection of Jesus as the cornerstone of faith. Here again Mark shows Jesus as servant leader.

Two key happenings in this section occur around meal tables. The first is the luxurious anointing of Jesus by an unnamed woman during a meal at Simon the leper's home (Mark 14:3-9). Additionally, the Lord's Supper pictures Jesus' celebration of the Passover with the twelve (Mark 14:12-31). Characteristic of Jewish custom as head of household, Jesus gave a homily on the meaning of the Passover. He, however, personalized his statements and paralleled the Passover elements with the impending sacrifice of his own body and blood (Mark 14:22-25). In this same context, Jesus told Simon Peter that he would betray Jesus (Mark 14:26-31).

In Gethsemane Jesus called on his intimate friends to support him with intercessory prayer during his emotional and spiritual crisis. An interesting contrast can be drawn between the fright felt during the storm on the sea (Mark 4:35-41) and the agony of Gethsemane. During the storm the disciples panicked and Jesus slept; in the garden Jesus was emotionally upset and the disciples slept. Apparently, Jesus saw more danger to the soul in the struggles with evil than in the perils of nature.

After his arrest Jesus was tried on trumped-up charges and condemned to die. In Mark's account this process moves quickly and includes few extra details. The point Mark intends to make is that salvation is offered to all because of the work of Christ. For instance, Simon of Cyrene, the women who stayed at the cross, Joseph of Arimathea, and the centurion discovered the central fact: the Cross opens the door to salvation for all who believe. In that fact, the Cross is both the power and proof of Jesus' servanthood.

Jesus' resurrection climaxes Mark's Gospel. With amazement and fear the women who discovered the empty tomb attempted to take in the supreme example of God's power. This servant of people and God who had been executed by the Romans and Jews had been given new life by God. He is risen. He is risen indeed. Christian leaders draw on the power of the servant who died but was raised to new service.

Servanthood as a Stance

More than a style of leadership, servanthood is a stance toward leadership shown in the Bible. A leadership stance provides a foundation, a basic position and reason for exercising leadership. Style, on the other hand, is a leader's manner of expressing initiative, a distinctive fashion of leading. Leader style is the theme of later essays in this book (see chapters 3–5).

Servanthood as a leader stance encouraged by biblical materials has several practical implications.

• *Servants lead out of relationships, not by coercion.* Servants don't demand obedience or submission. They meet their followers at the point of need. Servants have a common touch, maintain living contact, and demonstrate consistent concern for their followers.

• *Servants lead by support, not by control.* Servants give from themselves rather than take for themselves. They love and lift others rather than manipulating them.

• *Servants lead by developing others, not by doing all the ministry themselves.* Servants, whether clergy or laity, recognize that the kingdom of God calls for the full participation of all believers. All spiritual gifts are given by God for service to Christ's body (Eph. 4:11-13).

• *Servants guide people, not drive them.* Volunteer organizations like churches require selfless leaders rather than selfish bosses or bullies.

• *Servants lead from love, not domination.* Authority, in part, grows out of "the consent of the governed." Peter sounded this theme clearly: "Tend the flock of God that is your charge, not by constraint but willingly, not for shameful gain but eagerly, not as domineering over those in your charge but being examples to the flock" (1 Peter 5:2-3).

• *Servants seek growth, not position.* Servants aren't

ambitious. They keep the growth and spiritual health of others paramount. Unlike Diotrephes, an ambitious leader in the early church who preferred to "put himself first" (3 John 9), servants put others first.

Servanthood is obviously a demanding, high-risk leadership stance. But faith is demanding and risky too. Servanthood is full of crosses as well as towels and basins.

Overview: The Servant Leader Stance

Servanthood themes run throughout the Bible, especially the ministry of Jesus. Mark 10:35-45 is the best-known Synoptic passage about servant leadership, among many. Servanthood, however, is the most demanding approach Christians can take to leadership.

Review Questions

1. Can you list the primary leader groups in the Old Testament? The New Testament?
2. Can you describe Jesus as a servant leader?
3. Can you distinguish between a leadership stance and a leader style?

Notes

1. The biblical material on leadership is drawn from Robert D. Dale's *Ministers as Leaders* (Nashville: Broadman Press, 1984).
2. This perspective suggested by William R. Cannon's *Jesus the Servant: From the Gospel of Mark* (Nashville: Upper Room, 1978).

Selected Bibliography on Biblical Leadership

Dale, Robert D. *Ministers as Leaders* (Nashville: Broadman Press, 1984).

Dohan, Helen. *Leadership in Paul* (Wilmington, Del.: Michael Glazier, 1984).

Greenleaf, Robert K., *Servant Leadership* (Ramsey, N.J.: Paulist Press, 1977).

———. *The Servant as Religious Leader* (Peterborough, N.H.: Windy Row Press).

Mosley, Ernest E. ed. *Leadership Profiles from Bible Personalities* (Nashville: Broadman Press, 1979).

II.
Matching Leaders and Ministry Opportunities: Options

— 3 —

SELECTING YOUR
LEADER STYLE

THOMAS JEFFERSON ONCE observed that there are two kinds of leaders: those who trust people and those who fear people. While that division is a bit simplistic, Jefferson did spotlight one key for understanding leader styles: our theology of human nature. Our estimate of the impact of salvation and of the influence of sin on our followers shapes our leadership behaviors. If we feel salvation has freed us from the power of sin, we're apt to be a leader who gives freedom. Our theological assessment of human beings is directly expressed in our leader styles, and, is likely the most obvious daily expression of our theology in congregational ministry.

Do you basically trust or fear people? Trusting leaders are apt to be either partners and catalysts or nurturing encouragers. Fearful leaders are likely either to dictate their wishes to people or to avoid others altogether. Trust and fear underlie leader styles.

Style: What Is It?

Style is our characteristic manner of expressing our values and of executing our work. Style refers to our distinctive approach to others and our ministry. Each of us has a leader style. In some cases, we know our preferred pattern well. In other cases, those persons who work with us know our unrecognized style and can give us helpful feedback.

Styles: What Are Your Options?

The range of leader style options for ministers is virtually unlimited. For descriptive purposes, however, let's explore four mainstream possibilities: Catalysts, Commanders, Encouragers, and Hermits.[1]

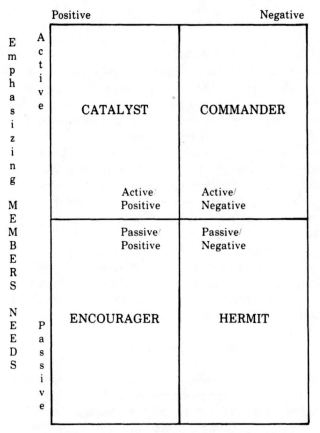

Illustration 6. *Congregational Leadership Model*

A model of pastoral leadership in congregations helps us visualize the options that are open to us. Note that this model emphasizes two essential dynamics for congregational effectiveness: mission goals and members' morale. The pursuit of mission can range from more positive, broadly based and widely owned goals to ends that are determined by leader choice alone (and, are in terms of congregational health, therefore, more negative). This provides the horizontal axis of the model. On the vertical axis, leaders can focus on the morale needs of members by more active, people-approaching initiatives or by behaviors that are more passive and less involved with persons.

Although none of us is likely to use any one of these styles in its pure form, let's draw each style option in stark terms to differentiate it from the others.

Catalyst: The Effective Style

Remember what a catalyst is in chemistry? It's an agent that causes or speeds a chemical reaction. The reaction doesn't, however, change the basic qualities of the catalyst. The same parallel holds for leader styles too. The Catalyst style of leader creates an organizational atmosphere in which positive goals are reached and people are built up actively. That dual focus explains why the Catalyst is the most effective style. Additionally, the Catalyst retains stability as a person and a professional.

What are the primary advantages of the active-positive Catalyst style?

● *The Catalyst is a balanced leader.* The evenhanded ability to keep leadership energies simultaneously aimed at both the congregation's mission and the needs of members is the basic strength of Catalysts. Catalysts integrate mission and morale, goals and persons' needs. Catalysts are realistic at one vital point—the Catalyst style demands a wider array of leader skills than any other style option.

4 1

• *The Catalyst is an active leader.* Leaders exercise initiative in relationships. They are able to approach people and demonstrate friendliness, vigor, and visibility.
• *The Catalyst is a positive leader.* The congregation's fundamental mission provides a beacon for Catalysts. They move forward steadily, patiently, and unswervingly. Why not? They know clearly what they stand for.
• *The Catalyst is a flexible leader.* The combination of positive goals and active, healthy relationships creates flexibility. Catalysts can deal with a broad range of ministry circumstances and a wide variety of personalities. Catalysts are participative and democratic leaders.
• *The Catalyst is a long-range leader.* Catalysts are patient planners and persistent implementers. They stick with their tasks and stand by their members. Catalysts train, activate, organize, and delegate to bring congregational goals to reality. Catalysts, to be effective, require a cadre of trained workers and the time for those workers to execute the plans of the congregation.

Building for the future is an attractive leadership characteristic. A traveler in Russia noted that piles of red wheat, seed for the next year's crop, were stacked in the open in every village in spite of widespread hunger. The visitor asked a farmer if he was ever tempted to eat some of the seed wheat. "Oh, no," replied the Russian. "You don't steal from the future!" That's a Catalyst perspective.

Commander: The Efficient Style

Commanders communicate their dictates clearly and cleanly. Then they expect others to follow the commands immediately. Because the leader is so sure of the proper course of action and followers are so clear about their options, the Commander leader style can be highly efficient. The Commander orders, and the follower obeys or leaves. Commanders are, like Catalysts, active, people-approachers. They are negative leaders, however, in the sense that they are apt to impose their own goals on the congregation. Commanders are directive, even auto-cratic. They put goals ahead of persons, production over relationships.

Why do Commanders behave so actively—even if their aggressive pattern of action doesn't match the demands of the situation? Maybe there's a clue in the basic principle of rehabilitative medicine: action overcomes anxiety. We may take some actions to alleviate our anxieties and uncertainties. Like my father used to tell me, "Do something—even if it's wrong!"

What are the main advantages of the active-negative Commander style?

- *The Commander is a leader whose demands are clearly defined.* Commanders know what they want; their followers know what's expected of them. It's a lean and clean leader-follower relationship. Commanders press for imme-diate action. They are kinetic personalities who believe quick, simple answers can be found to every problem.
- *The Commander leader has a narrow agenda.* Com-manders set the range of actions to be taken by the congregation. Commanders determine what will be done, when, and by whom.
- *The Commander mindset tends to be rigid.* The leader-follower relationship is tightly defined in this pattern. Commanders make the task and authority structure abundantly clear. Followers have little latitude for responding.
- *The Commander style is a short-range one.* Quick results and immediate reactions are possible when Commanders are in charge. The high-structure nature of the Com-mander style adapts itself well to emergency situations. Emergencies, by definition, are rarely ongoing; the Commander responds to most circumstances in a fashion that fits emergencies well but other situations poorly.
- *The Commander leader style creates pressure and conflict.* Commanders' directive behavior keeps expecta-tions high and promotes a we-versus-they atmosphere.

Commanders, unlike Encouragers, are slow to learn Carnes' Canon: "Never use a bullwhip when a smile will do it better."[2]

Social psychologist Carol Tavris, writing from the ethnic and religious background of eastern European Judaism, claims that the "have dominion" passage of Genesis 1:26 coupled with the harsh desert climate in which Israel's theological perspective was developed created an "active pessimism."[3] This stance, similar to the Commander's set of assumptions, yields an aggressive, organizational culture and a directive attitude toward life and leadership.

Encourager: The Empathetic Style

An Encourager emphasizes personal relationships more than organizational goals, morale over mission. If Commanders have adopted their view of a corporate officer's work style, Encouragers have made the therapist's role into a leadership approach. Encouragers hold hands, pat heads, give strokes, and generally give top priority to relational needs. They get little satisfaction from organizational efforts and, therefore, invest little energy in congregational goals—except for fellowship goals.

Anthropologist Robert Levy claims that a culture like that of Tahiti creates a "relax and accept the bounties of nature" mindset.[4] This lifestyle promotes a "passive optimism" akin to the Encourager's leader style.

What are the advantages of the passive-positive Encourager leader style?

• *The Encourager leader is a person-centered minister.* Encouragers listen well, are available to members, and work to enrich fellowship. They are permissive where people are concerned. Encouragers nurture others, soothe them, and empathize with their hurts.
• *The Encourager leader makes production a secondary concern.* The good news is that the leader's focus isn't divided. The bad news is that the congregation's broader goals aren't pursued as aggressively as relational issues.

Encouragers are nondirective—they leave both the organizational and relational agendas in others' hands. As a result, congregational organizations are left untended and tangible production wanes.

● *The Encourager leader style fits nicely in congregations who are experiencing member stress and congregational conflict.* Encouragers create relaxed atmospheres, bind people together, mediate differences, and build up morale.

Hermit: The Eroding Style

The Hermit is uncomfortable with both people and goals. Consequently, Hermits withdraw from people and abandon organizational initiatives to the congregation's self-starters. Whether naturally shy or made into Hermits by congregational abuse, they postpone, hide, and generally signal uncertainty. Hermit leaders actually follow their followers. Their submissive behavior is probably designed for personal safety but more often yields an inert congregation.

What are the advantages of the passive-negative Hermit leader style?

● *The Hermit leader style can buy valuable decision-making time when the congregational climate is tense and polarizing.* The Hermit leader's reticence to deal with people or goals may allow sides to table their differences long enough to search for better solutions.

● *The Hermit leader style allows for time out for rest and recreation.* If, however, the Hermit style is adopted as a day-in, day-out approach, nothing happens in the organization, and the leader is also left vulnerable.

Extending Basic Styles

Did you identify your primary style? Probably none of us leads out of one style exclusively. We're likely mixtures of the basic styles anyway. Elements in the leadership situation may cause us to adopt some behaviors of other styles. Here are some examples of how we extend from our usual style into the ones "next door."

Catalysts may adopt some Commander and Encourager behaviors. These actions expand the zone of effectiveness for Catalyst ministers.

Catalysts May
Extend into Commander Behaviors

—Press for goals persistently
—Assert own vision strongly.
—Settle for short-term gains.

CATALYST	COMMANDER
ENCOURAGER	HERMIT

Catalysts May Extend into Encourager Behaviors

—Negotiate intergroup differences.
—Heal organizational schisms.
—Work well with cliques.

Illustration 7. Catalyst Style Extensions.

Commanders may take on some Catalyst and Hermit behaviors.

Commanders May
Extend into Hermit Behaviors

—Retreat to rest from intensity.
—Withdraw to sulk over defeat.
—Use silence as a bargaining tool

CATALYST	COMMANDER
ENCOURAGER	HERMIT

Commanders May Extend into Catalyst Behaviors

—Become a temporary team player for the sake of a goal.
—Use projects as a mechanism to pursue longer-range goals.
—Develop people in order to support goals.

Illustration 8. Commander Style extensions.

Encouragers may practice some Catalyst and Hermit behaviors.

Encouragers May Extend into
Hermit Behaviors

—Pull back from people to lick wounds.
—Lean on followers for organizational leadership
—Postpone action, especially organizational initiatives.

CATALYST	COMMANDER
ENCOURAGER	HERMIT

Encouragers May Extend into Catalyst Behaviors

—Support leadership persons in the congregation.
—Show a degree of interest in congregational health.
—Pursue fellowship goals.

Illustration 9. Encourager Style Extensions.

Hermits may fall back into some Commander and Encourager behaviors.

Hermits May Extend into
Commander Behaviors

—Stiffen resistance for self-protection.
—Demonstrate rigidity.

CATALYST	COMMANDER
ENCOURAGER	HERMIT

Hermits May
Extend into
Encourager Behaviors.

—Pursue selective relationships.
—Become a keen student of human nature.

Illustration 10. Hermit Style Extensions.

Blends of Basic Styles

Another variation on the basic style themes involves style blends. Note two possibilities: the Entrepreneur and the Harmonizer.

The Entrepreneur blend overlaps the general boundary area between the Catalyst and Commander styles. Entrepreneurs are dreamers, organizers, risk takers, and builders. Some church growth movement theorists seem to favor this style blend. Entrepreneurs prefer to launch new enterprises or projects rather than to maintain them. In America's secular culture, this style blend is also currently in vogue. Futurist John Naisbitt claims in *Megatrends,* "We are shifting from a managerial society to an entrepreneurial society."[5] The style and spirit of the Entrepreneur appears again in *Time* magazine's choice of Peter Ueberroth, the organizer of the Los Angeles Olympics, as its 1984 Man of the Year.[6]

The Harmonizer blend overlaps the Catalyst and Encourager styles. This style blend spotlights people within goals. Harmonizers are friendly, agreeable, and peaceable in relationships. They are orderly leaders who are adept at combining varied ideas and interests into working arrangements. Harmonizers are skillful negotiators. Administratively, they prefer managing existing organizations over starting new units.

Identifying Your Back-up Style

Extending your primary leader style or using a blended style is a conscious behavior generally. Back-up styles are another matter, however.[7] Back-up styles are unconscious style switches we make under pressure. We use our back-up style for survival purposes. Like the caveman who found himself confronted by a saber-toothed tiger in some jungle clearing, in emergency situations we too either fight or flee. In other words, under extreme pressure our

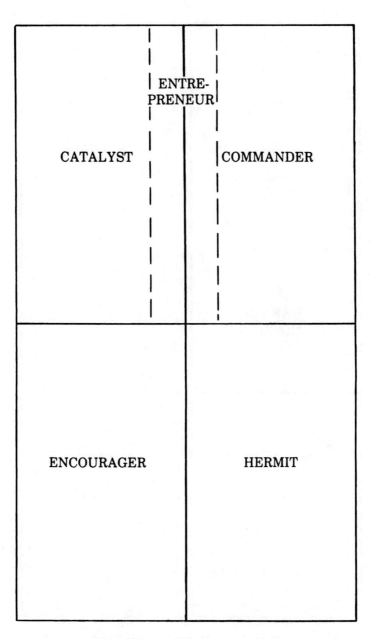

Ilustration 11. Entrepreneur Style Blend

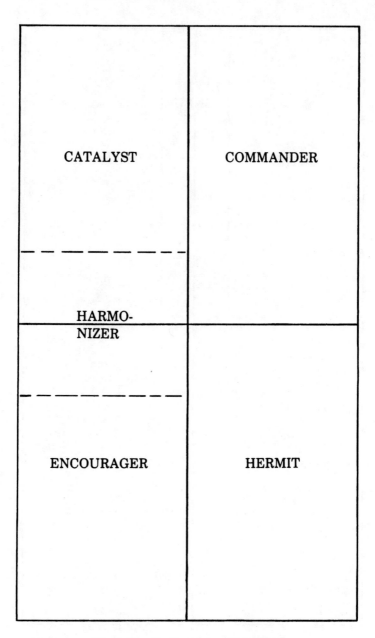

Illustration 12. Harmonizer Style Blend

primary leader style automatically shifts either toward much more or drastically less structure.

What are the most likely back-up style adjustments? Catalysts may increase structure and become Commanders or lessen structure and focus on Encourager behaviors. Commanders may open up to participative Catalyst actions or retreat into Hermit-hood. Encouragers may add organizational emphasis and become Catalysts or withdraw like Hermits. Hermits may rise up like Commanders or increase their ability to take the relational risks of Encouragers. Of course, when the situational stress runs its course, we revert to our primary leader style pattern.

Leader Style: One of Three

The leader's style is one of three elements of organizational effectiveness. We've described leader style options here. The other two ingredients—the followers' style and the demands of the particular ministry situation—are the focus of chapter 4.

Overview: Leader Styles

Congregational leaders can stress either the mission of the organization or the morale needs of members. Descriptively, ministry leaders can be termed as Catalysts, Commanders, Encouragers, and Hermits. Basic leader styles can be extended or blended. Moreover, emergency circumstances often trigger our back-up styles.

Review Questions

1. Can you describe Catalyst leaders? Commanders? Encouragers? Hermits?
2. Can you identify and describe two blended leadership styles?
3. As a leader, is your back-up style more structured or less structured than your usual style?

Notes

1. Robert D. Dale, *Ministers as Leaders* (Nashville: Broadman Press, 1984). All rights reserved. Used by permission.
2. William T. Carnes, *Effective Meetings for Busy People* (New York: McGraw-Hill, 1980), p. 11.
3. Carol Tavris, *Anger: The Misunderstood Emotion* (New York: Simon & Schuster, 1983), p. 63.
4. Ibid.
5. John Naisbitt, *Megatrends* (New York: Warner Books, 1982), p. 149.
6. *Time*, January 7, 1985, pp.32-39.
7. Dale, *Ministers as Leaders*, pp. 65-66.

Selected Bibliography on Leader Styles

Barber, James David. *The Presidential Character* (Englewood Cliffs, N.J.: Prentice-Hall, 1977).

Bennis, Warren. *The Unconscious Conspiracy* (New York: AMACOM, 1976).

Burns, James MacGregor. *Leadership* (New York: Harper & Row, 1978).

Dale, Robert D. *Ministers as Leaders* (Nashville: Broadman Press, 1984).

Engstrom, Ted W. *The Making of a Christian Leader* (Grand Rapids: Zondervan Corp., 1976).

Greenleaf, Robert K. *Servant Leadership* (Ramsey, N.J.: Paulist Press, 1977).

Keating, Charles J. *The Leadership Book*, rev. ed. (Ramsey, N.J.: Paulist Press, 1978).

Mosley, Ernest E. ed., *Leadership Profiles from Bible Personalities* (Nashville: Broadman Press, 1979).

— 4 —

THE
LEADERSHIP TRIANGLE:
A MINISTRY CHALLENGE

YEARS AGO A small burro had an unusual task on one of the vast cattle ranches in the American West. The burro's job was to tame the wildest steers. The burro and a steer were tied together and turned loose in the desert. The steer would discover the tether in a few moments and bolt across the range dragging the little burro behind him like a streamer in the wind. But, try as he would, the steer couldn't shake the burro. Eventually, the steer would give in and give up. A few hours or days later the little burro would return home with the steer firmly in tow.

There are some lessons for leaders in this story. First, leaders and followers function as a team or not at all. Second, leaders learn how to cope with their circumstances and settings. Third, the heroes of God's kingdom are more apt to be determined than dramatic.

Leadership in congregational settings is relational and interactive in its focus. After all, the leader isn't the only member of the community. There are followers' preferences and the full range of ministry demands and circumstances to consider. Leadership isn't exercised in isolation. Leaders and followers relate to one another; leaders and situations interact.[1]

Leadership in congregations is an interactive triangle.[2] Effective leaders recognize the three elements of this triangle: (1) their own preferred and comfortable leader style, (2) the comfortable relational styles of their followers, and (3) the most productively structured ministry situations for them. Pastoral leaders are alert to the most comfortable and productive combination of these three elements—leader-follower-situation.

Is this leadership triangle too complex to analyze? No. Leaders can select their own leader style and can help structure the ministry situations they work in. In other words, leaders can influence two of the three points of the leadership triangle. That creates favorable, reciprocal, and complementary possibilities for effective leadership. Leaders can't determine their followers' style reactions, however, unless they choose to manipulate.

Leader-Follower Patterns: One Side of the Triangle

Followers develop styles of relating to leaders. Followers, like leaders, also choose their styles from the full range of emotional responses. The model below notes that church members draw meaning from their institutional community and have an expectation that leaders will enrich their lives in some significant way.

Community of Meaning

E n r i c h i n g L i f e		
PARTICIPANT (gains both meaning and enrichment from leader)	DEPENDENT (counts on leader for meaning primarily)
RECEIVER (counts on leader for enrichment primarily)	SELF-STARTER (gains little meaning or enrichment from leader)

Illustration 13. Follower Style Model

Leader-Situation Patterns:
Another Side of the Triangle

Another side of the leadership triangle, the leader's ability to recognize and adjust to the demands of ministry situations, completes the leadership mesh challenge. Ministry is done in a variety of circumstances, some tightly structured and others hardly defined at all. By the same token, leaders and followers are comfortable with various degrees of structure.

Ministry situations are generally structured by two dynamics: the congregation's institutional resources and the initiative or structure leaders themselves bring to ministry. Note the continuum of ministry situations below and how they relate to the leader-situation mix.

Organizational Resources

S
t
r
u
c
t
u
r
i
n
g

H
e
l
p

COOPERATIVE SITUATIONS (draws on both congregational resources and leader's structure)	UNSTABLE and OVERSTABLE SITUATIONS (relies on leader for organizational resources primarily)
ORDERLY SITUATIONS (relies on leader for helpful structure primarily)	SELF-SUSTAINING SITUATIONS (draws only marginally on congregational resources and leader's structure)

Illustration 14. Ministry Situations Model

Effective pastoral leaders make ministry situations their servant rather than their dictator. Former British prime minister Disraeli observed, "Man is not the creature of circumstance, circumstances are the creatures of men." That's a helpful reminder when analyzing the leadership triangle.

Catalysts' Triangles: Participant Followers and Cooperative Situations

The most productive mix for Catalyst leaders incorporates followers with a participative stance and cooperative ministry circumstances. These three aspects of leadership in congregations complement one another well. We have already described the Catalyst style and will now explore the Participant Follower and the Cooperative Ministry Situations.

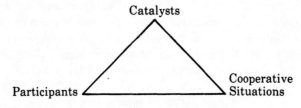

Illustration 15. Catalyst Mix

Participant followers feel strongly about the congregation's ministry dream and commit their best efforts to making that dream become reality. Participants also contribute to the overall morale level of the congregation. In fact, wholehearted support of and involvement in the congregation's vision of ministry and its membership morale needs set the stage for participant followers to develop into leaders also.

Participant followers are team players because of their psychological ownership of the congregation's enterprises. Participants are cooperative, active, and sharing partners. They join in all the congregation's ministry processes—dreaming, planning, deciding, setting goals, enriching fellowship, and implementing ministry actions.

Cooperative ministry situations offer plentiful resources for the projects the congregation dreams of and chooses. The congregation has clear goals, and the leader provides the needed structure to pursue mission and to care for members.

What ingredients are most favorable for the combination of the Catalyst-Participant-Cooperative Situation?

- Adequate resources are available for teamwork.
- A cluster of trained, willing workers is ready for involvement.
- Enough time and patience are present to pursue longer-range goals.
- Ministry settings in which mass participation is indicated are present.
- The congregation's membership is heterogeneous and pluralistic.
- Long-range goals are at stake.
- The congregation has a reasonable degree of clarity about its dream and direction.

Commanders' Triangles: Dependent Followers and Either Unstable or Overstable Situations

Commanders relate most comfortably with followers who are dependent personalities and ministry situations that are either unstable and shaky or overstable and stuck. Let's examine the Commander-Dependent-Unstable/Overstable Situation ministry combination.

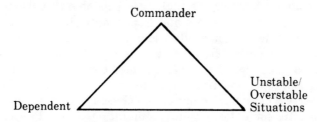

Illustration 16. Commander Mix

Dependents prefer to make "follow the leader" more than a child's game. They like the protection the Commander's directives provide; they enjoy the high degree of structure the Commander's personality supplies. Dependents are, therefore, comfortable as helpers and powers behind the throne. These loyal lieutenants choose to move quietly; they avoid decision-making and direct responsibility, organizational visibility, and assertive action. Dependents, in their most extreme forms, become puppets and can be easily manipulated.

The combination of the Commander's forcefulness or charisma and the Dependent's reliance on others for personal definition can create an "authoritarian dyad,"[3] a relationship in which the domineering leader and the helpless follower feed off each other. The leader gains control, and the follower avoids risk and responsibility in this symbiotic relationship. The shortcomings of this leader-follower link are that (1) neither the Commander nor the Dependent develops an authentic relationship, and (2) no new leaders are grown for the future. Power wielders typically feel lonely because they do not see peers for themselves, and they sense the heavy burden of authority because they don't trust others with delegated responsibility.

From the perspective of ministry setting, unstable ministry situations fit this leadership triangle well. Unstable circumstances feature emergency or shaky predicaments. Confusion, chaos, and panic lead to a loss of organizational or personal control. Commanders and Dependents function well in these Unstable Situations; Commanders give orders and Dependents obey.

Overstable ministry situations also match the Commander-Dependent link nicely. Stagnant or stuck organizations and apathetic church members create inert congregations. Inertia, according to physicists, is the property which makes motionless objects remain stationary until some force puts them into motion. Physics reminds us that the greater the mass of these inert objects, the more difficult it is to put these objects into motion or to change their direction. When ministry leaders encounter inert situations, they may adopt a Commander stance temporarily to nudge the congregation into action.

Note the ingredients necessary for a comfortable

Commander-Dependent-Unstable/Overstable Situation match.

- Emergency or chaotic circumstances reign.
- Dependent personalities make up the congregation.
- The congregation is stuck, and its inertia must be confronted.
- Quick, short-term results are desired.
- Lots of structure is warranted.
- Production is more important than people.

Encouragers' Triangles: Receiver Followers and Orderly Situations

Encouragers prefer followers who receive their encouragement eagerly and orderly situations which require a minimum of their time and attention. Encouragers enjoy relationships more than organizational or mission tasks. Consider the Encourager-Receiver-Orderly Situation ministry triangle.

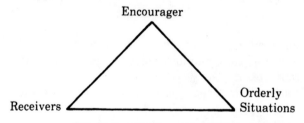

Illustration 17. Encourager Mix

Receivers enjoy the fellowship of the congregation, or at least, groups within it. They are frequently less ardent about the broader missional goals of the congregation, however. Receivers want to belong and to be cared for emotionally. They need and often demand close attention from, as well as general relationships with, Encouragers. The leader and some portion of the congregation's membership provide the Receiver's primary relationships.

Encouragers may overreact to the relational needs of Receivers and become too protective. When this reaction occurs, Encouragers are apt to spoil Receivers and create a relationship of mutual need between them. This "teacher and teacher's pet" link doesn't allow the Receivers to grow into bona fide leaders either. The Encourager-Receiver match emphasizes people over production and, therefore, is more likely to result in congregational fellowship rather than mission advance. Receivers, comfortable in this setting, can enjoy fellowship, pursue the congregational goals they select, or relax and do nothing.

Orderly ministry circumstances are the preferences of Encouragers simply because they would rather focus on relational concerns than on congregational goals. When steady, well designed organizational structures exist, Encouragers can concentrate on creating a warm, supportive, and relaxed atmosphere. They can then zero in on preaching, teaching, and counseling while counting on the structures of the congregation to guide the administrative needs of the church.

The Encourager-Receiver-Orderly Situation mix thrives on an array of ingredients.

- Relational and fellowship issues are paramount.
- Emotional calm and lower organizational priorities are appropriate.
- Emotional breaches need to be healed in the congregation.
- Production can be put on hold.
- Organizational routines are in place and can be relied on to provide congregational structure.

Hermits' Triangles: Self-starting Followers and Self-sustaining Situations

Hermits need followers who are Self-starters to relate to. Likewise, they prefer congregational structures that are Self-sustaining. The combination of Hermits matched with Self-starters and Self-sustaining organizations deserves a closer look.

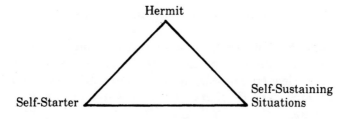

Illustration 18. Hermit Mix

Self-starters get an adequate sense of identity and service from the congregation's mission and members. This is a fortunate result because, other than a symbolic presence, the Hermit leader doesn't lead. In fact, Hermits may actually follow the Self-starters in their congregations. Self-starters, like nature, abhor a vacuum, and, therefore, move into the gap left by Hermits' passive inaction. Hermits pull back; Self-starters exercise their initiative independently and act out of their own motivation.

Self-sustaining programs and projects fit Hermits' leadership bent well. Ministry that operates on autopilot appeals to Hermits because organizational maintenance demands for them are virtually eliminated. Hermits prefer a minimum of people and/or organizational requirements.

Several ingredients set the stage for the Hermit and Self-starter and Self-sustaining Situations mix.

• Polarizing congregations may choose to put their tough decisions on hold for a stated period of time in order to search for better solutions than the ones they are considering.
• Leader burnout, by either clergy or laity or both, may call for time out to recharge emotional batteries.
• When congregational conflict approaches the breaking

point, adopting a "hands off" stance in order to let cooler heads prevail may be wise.

The Challenge of Leadership

Leaders. Followers. Situations. It's a challenge to find productive ministry matches. But the puzzle can be solved because leaders can learn to (1) recognize all three factors in the mix and (2) shape two of the three factors in the triangle.

Overview: Leadership Mesh Factors

Leader style, follower style, and ministry situation make up the three sides of the leadership triangle. Followers, like leaders, develop a style pattern. These style preferences include Participants, Dependents, Receivers, and Self-starters. Leaders and followers discover ministry situations with varying amounts of structure comfortable for them.

Review Questions

1. Can you identify the three interactive elements of the leadership triangle?
2. Can you describe the basic follower style patterns?
3. Can you list the basic types of ministry situations leaders prefer?
4. Can you match up the most compatible leadership triangles?

Notes

1. Robert D. Dale, *Ministers as Leaders* (Nashville: Broadman Press, 1984), pp. 55-69. All rights reserved. Used by permission.
2. Daniel A. Tagliere, *People, Power, and Organization* (New York: AMACOM, 1973).
3. Maria Carmen Gear, Ernesto Cesar Liendo, and Lila Lee Scott, *Patients and Agents* (New York: Jason Aronson, 1983), pp.22-44.

Selected Bibliography on Situational Leadership

Bolton, Robert. *People Skills*. Englewood Cliffs, N.J.: Prentice-Hall, 1979.

Burns, James MacGregor. *Leadership*. New York: Harper & Row, 1978.

Dale, Robert D. *Ministers as Leaders*. Nashville: Broadman Press, 1984.

Fiedler, Fred E., and Chemers, Martin M. *Improving Leadership Effectiveness: The Leader Match Concept*. New York: John Wiley & Sons, 1976.

"Leadership and Followership: Changing Conditions and Styles." A special issue of the *Journal of Applied Behavioral Science* 18, no. 3 (1982).

Tagliere, Daniel A. *People, Power, and Organization*. New York: AMACOM, 1973.

BIBLICAL MODELS OF LEADER STYLES

ONE WAY TO examine theoretical models for ministry is to see if they square with biblical examples. Can we find persons who led as Catalysts, Commanders, Encouragers, and Hermits in the mainstream of the biblical record? Did these leaders' styles mesh well with their followers and the historic situations they faced?

Yes, the Bible describes a rich variety of leaders. While the primary leader style of biblical characters isn't always easy to determine, some cases are reasonably clear. Nehemiah, Esther, and Paul are biblical possibilities for the Catalyst category. The judges, Moses during his early ministry, and David illustrate the Commander leader style. Barnabas, Andrew, and Ruth provide instances of the Encourager type leader. King Saul during the later years of his reign, Jeremiah, and the sages fit the Hermit style of leader.

Each of the four styles will be explored using biblical personalities. Nehemiah, the judges, Barnabas, and King Saul provide biblical illustrations of the four-style model of leadership.

Nehemiah: Catalyst Leader

The biblical book of Nehemiah begins with a sob and ends with a shout of joy. The story that unfolds between the weeping and the celebration is a fascinating saga of catalytic leadership. Popular recollection recalls Nehemiah as the restorer of Jerusalem's walls; a more balanced view reveals Nehemiah as a builder of both walls and people.[1]

Nehemiah led in beginning a restoration process for a nation in exile.[2] Under the domination of the Persians, the city wall of Jerusalem and the Jewish worship practices had broken down. Nehemiah used two resources—a divine calling and the political and economic assistance of King Artaxerxes—to turn the situation around. This layman exercised a pivotal ministry of city management.

Typical of Catalysts, Nehemiah integrated his vision and his concern for people. He had a head full of goals and a heart full of empathy. People and walls—they sum up the catalytic issues in Nehemiah's life. Note the dual emphases of Nehemiah's leadership efforts. On the mission or production side of his leadership, Nehemiah had a vision of a restored community. He dreamed of rebuilding the city wall of Jerusalem and restoring the religious practices of the people. On the morale or relational side of Nehemiah's leader style, he demonstrated his concern for others in weeping over the plight of Jerusalem's citizens, serving as food taster for the king, and organizing for the defense of Jerusalem's residents. Mission coupled with morale. A balance between production and people. That's the mix in Nehemiah's leader style—walls and people.

A recent study has identified the characteristics of "Super Leaders."[3] Super Leaders like Nehemiah not only demonstrate self-leadership skills but promote them in their followers. Modeling is the first Super Leader characteristic. They set goals and act on them, show their work is enjoyable, and concentrate on taking initiative, finding solutions, and creating opportunities. Secondly, Super Leaders develop and encourage their followers. For example, they ask good questions that help followers discover their own answers and resources, and, thereby, learn to lead themselves. Finally, when followers begin to practice self-leadership, Super Leaders give positive reinforcement for constructive actions, offer feedback, make suggestions, and, above all, show an optimistic attitude. These three characteristics are apparent in Nehemiah, the Catalyst.

Let's look at an illustrative catalog of three of Nehemiah's modeling actions. Here he clearly demonstrated how his followers could practice leadership themselves.

One: Nehemiah took the risk of stating his case directly to the king. Nehemiah was "very much afraid" (Neh. 2:2) as he described his sadness to Artaxerxes. But his risk taking was rewarded by the king's support in the rebuilding of Jerusalem.

Two: Nehemiah planned carefully. He knew that he would need political support in order to succeed when others had failed (Ezra 4). He secured the necessary construction materials (Neh. 2:7-8). He scouted the construction site and sized up specific needs (Neh. 2:11-16). He developed an orderly building plan that guided the step-by-step sequence of refurbishing the walls in a counterclockwise fashion (Neh. 3:3-32). He provided for the defense of the city (Neh. 4:13-23). He renewed worship and the Jewish traditions (Neh. 13:4-29). Through the entire process Nehemiah worked as hard and long, but more visibly, than any of the others.

Three: Nehemiah refused to fellowship with the enemies of Jerusalem. His priorities were clear. Whether his enemies intended to ambush him or merely to charm and distract him from his central task isn't clear. But Nehemiah's response is straightforward: "I am doing a great work and I cannot come down" (Neh. 6:3).

Additionally, like other Super Leaders, Nehemiah built up his followers into leaders. Obviously he could build an effective work team. Rebuilding the city's wall in fifty-two days testifies to Nehemiah's abilities as a team leader, a morale maintainer, and a healthy group climate developer (Neh. 3; 4:15-23). Moreover, Nehemiah was able to delegate effectively, and, thereby, share his burdens while also developing future leaders.

One characteristic of Nehemiah that helped him empathize with others was his ability for "both-and" thinking. Both men and women joined in the rebuilding efforts. All kinds of skilled and unskilled persons offered their energies to the restorative enterprise. He united both the folks who lived inside the ruined walls and those who resided outside the city. He combined building and defending activities. These both-and solutions indicate Nehemiah's breadth and flexibility. Since no one felt overlooked or unimportant, all apparently felt included and supported.

Lastly, Nehemiah gave positive reinforcement well. Most notable in this connection was the celebration he designed to help the residents signify their dependence on God in rebuilding the wall. So great were their festivities that "the joy of Jerusalem was heard afar off" (Neh. 12:43). Joy is often the emotion that balanced Catalysts awaken in their followers.

The Judges: Commander Leaders

Crisis episodes call for Commander leaders, literally. It's no surprise, then, that the judges of the Old Testament were consistently Commander style leaders. The emergency situations for which they provided structure demanded high degrees of directiveness.

Several characteristics mark the judges as leaders. Notice that the historical circumstances the judges encountered were trying times and turning points for the fledgling Israelite nation.

● They served during extreme eras of the history of Israel's tribes. They functioned between the uncertain times of Joshua and the rise of the prophet Samuel. The judges helped deliver the local tribes from destructive

cycles of sin, idolatry, and apostasy. Four stages characterized the period of the judges: sin, oppression, deliverance,
and faithfulness. Some of the Israelites were drawn to the
gaudy "sophistication" of the Canaanite Baals (Judg.
6:25-32). Falling into the sin of Baal worship would trigger
the down-then-up cycle of the judges (Judg. 2:16-18a). The
cycle would finally run its course, and Israel would remain
faithful to God while they were led by a judge (Judg.
2:18b).

• The judges were military heroes and heroines of their
individual tribes and clans. They weren't officers of the
law. There wasn't, of course, any form of centralized
government in Israel yet. They were local and tribal, not
national, leaders.

• They were inspirational and charismatic leaders, not
heirs of any royal lineage. The judges numbered about a
half-dozen major personages with roughly an equal
number of minor figures.

• The judges were interim rescuers. They were probably
chosen by the tribal leaders and served only as long as they
were effective and needed. They, therefore, were temporary guides rather than permanent ones. To illustrate,
after Gideon's triumphs, he retired from his leadership of
the army and returned home (Judg. 8:22-35).

• The judges often served concurrently instead of consecu-
tively. Consequently, the judges' terms of service often
overlapped each other or left gaps of leaderlessness
between their eras.

• The major judges faced different enemies from the
Canaanite and Philistine city-states. Interestingly, they
are only described as belonging to the northern tribes.

• The methods of deliverance used by the judges included
battle (by Othniel, Gideon, and Abimelech among others),
assassination (by Deborah and Barak as well as Benja-
min), and revenge (by Samson). Common to the judges are
the exploits of brave men and women who led by
individual acts of physical and spiritual prowess. For
example, Ehud, acting as the deliverer of tribute pay-

ments, used his left-handedness to his advantage. He hid a sword under the right side of his robe and dispatched Eglon, the unsuspecting Moabite king. Or, Jael, a Gentile woman leader, who assassinated Sisera with an improvised Bedouin weapon, a tent peg (Judg. 5:26-27).

• The judges weren't always prime examples of morality. On occasion they lied, showed hatred and cruelty, were sexually immoral, and, of course, killed. Samson, for instance, was hardly a paragon of virtue. During the so-called Dark Ages of Israel's history, they demonstrated the struggles of a new nation trying to identify and live out its religious uniqueness. Intriguingly, the Joshua-Judges stories contain sparse reference to prophets (Judg. 6:8-10).

Like many Commanders, the judges "got the job done." Their enemies were at least temporarily dispersed. However, new leaders weren't developed, the nation wasn't unified, and the future wasn't secured. The judges, typical of Commanders, succeeded only in the short term.

Barnabas: Encourager Leader

"Son of encouragement." That's the nickname applied to Joseph Barnabas the first time he appears in the pages of the New Testament (Acts 4:36). The Encourager label continued to fit Barnabas and his leader style throughout the rest of the biblical record. Barnabas, a Levite and a Cypriot, was able to bridge the Jewish-Christian and Gentile worlds and provide leadership for the budding missionary movement.[4]

The brief statements about him in the Bible describe Barnabas as a people-oriented leader. Note these trends in the leader style of Barnabas.

• Barnabas had a gift for developing friendships. The Barnabas story is a saga of friendliness. Remember these scenes in the Encourager's life?

Scene one: Barnabas befriended Paul when the converted Paul returned to Jerusalem and tried to join the Christian community there, the believers were suspicious of him. How was this disbelief overcome? Barnabas interceded and "brought him to the apostles, and declared to them how on the road he had seen the Lord, who spoke to him, and how at Damascus he had preached boldly in the name of Jesus. So he went in and out among them at Jerusalem, preaching boldly in the name of the Lord" (Acts 9:27-29a). Paul was accepted into the Jerusalem church because Barnabas befriended him and vouched for him.

Scene two: Barnabas supported new Christians. Persecution scattered the early Christian community. Some of these Christians settled in Antioch and preached there. New converts resulted from their missionary work; the believers were first called Christians here. The news of an emerging Christian community in Antioch reached Jerusalem. The Jerusalem church sent Barnabas to encourage the new believers in Antioch. When Barnabas arrived and "saw the grace of God, he was glad; and he exhorted them all to remain faithful to the Lord with steadfast purpose; for he was a good man, full of the Holy Spirit and of faith" (Acts 11:23-24). Later Barnabas enlisted the well-educated Paul to assist him in teaching the new Christians. Barnabas' Christian friendship supported these new believers.

Scene three: Barnabas responded to the needy.—When word arrived in Antioch that famine was spreading through Judea, the Christians at Antioch sent Barnabas and Paul to deliver an offering to those in need (Acts 11:27-30). Barnabas cared for others and was trustworthy in handling money.

Scene four: Barnabas believed in John Mark.—The Antioch church commissioned Barnabas and Paul to go on the first Christian missionary effort. John Mark, a young relative of Barnabas, accompanied the pair. However, John Mark turned back (Acts 13:13).

When the second missionary journey was about to be launched, Barnabas wanted to take John Mark along again, but Paul refused emphatically (Acts 15:37-39).

Barnabas and Paul split up, and Barnabas took Mark as his new partner. Mark showed himself a competent evangelist, and Paul later wanted Mark to work with him again (2 Tim. 4:11). Since none of us is perfect, we need and appreciate our friends with Barnabas' ability to give others a second chance.

What's the result of Barnabas' gift of friendship? Let's use our imaginations a bit and read between the lines. In one sense, because Barnabas was a consistent friend, he became the author of two-thirds of the New Testament. Not literally, of course. But consider this scenario. Barnabas vouched for Paul, and then Paul wrote roughly half of the New Testament. Moreover, Barnabas gave Mark another chance, and later Mark authored the earliest Gospel, the eyewitness account of Jesus' ministry as seen by Simon Peter. Ninety percent of Mark's Gospel shows up in both Matthew and Luke's Gospels. Add the impact of Paul and Mark's writing efforts together, and you can see how Barnabas' fingerprints are on a majority of the pages of the New Testament.

• Barnabas was generous with needy believers. Barnabas' initial appearance in the New Testament record shows his generosity. The members of the early church cared for the practical, physical needs of one another. In contrast to the devious actions of Ananias and Sapphira, Barnabas showed great-heartedness by selling some of his personal property and giving it to the church (Acts 4:32-37). He didn't hesitate to give freely to meet the needs of other believers.

• Barnabas managed conflict effectively. The disagreement between Barnabas and Paul over whether Mark would accompany them on the second missionary journey was apparently keener than some interpreters note. The Bible refers to the two leaders' rift as "a sharp contention" (Acts 15:39). Rather than allow the missionary enterprise to be crippled by their conflict, they simply formed two missionary teams. They found a win-win resolution. Barnabas' evaluation regarding John Mark was later confirmed in Paul's writings. Paul sends Mark's greeting to fellow Christians (Col. 4:10) and notes that Mark is his fellow worker (Philem. 23-24). Effective leadership finds ways to keep the natural conflict experienced by persons with strong convictions from wounding the broader Christian enterprise.

• Barnabas was a trusted negotiator. Missionary work introduced an interesting and important question into the theology of the Christian movement: Did converts have to become Jews before they could become Christians? Barnabas and Paul held that the grace of Christ alone was sufficient for those who wished to become Christians; others demanded that converts become ritual Jews first and then accept Christ. A council was called in Jerusalem, and there Barnabas and Paul reported the results of their work in Gentile territories. The entire assembly listened to the witness of Barnabas and Paul "as they related what signs and wonders God had done through them among the Gentiles" (Acts 15:12). Mutual trust, the ability to listen sensitively, and the conviction to state beliefs clearly set the stage for effective group decision-making.

Barnabas exhibits the Encourager leader style consistently. Throughout the biblical record, in typical Encourager fashion, he invites relationships somewhat more than he pushes for production. In "people work" Barnabas was an effective leader.

Saul: Hermit Leader

Saul was a leader with great promise. He was a tall, handsome, and wealthy Benjaminite. Saul became Israel's first king. But by the end of his reign, he had fallen into a classic Hermit leader style pattern. His prime goal was personal survival, and he trusted no one.

The question of whether or not Israel needed a king created a difference of opinion in the nation. For some, the monarchy was a necessity. For others, a king represented apostasy.

The uncertainty generated by the office of king appears in Deuteronomy 12–26, the constitution for Israel's theocratically oriented life. Here the office of king is a possibility, not an order (Deut. 17:14-15a). However, any king was to be an Israelite, in order to reduce the possibility of worshiping foreign gods (Deut. 17:15b). Additionally, kings were to be wary of foreign alliances and were to remain students of the law.

At the close of the period of the judges, Israel was still facing a series of crises. 1 Samuel 8:1-22, then, tells of the people's demand for a king, a leader to unite the nation for military purposes. The people begged Samuel, "Behold, you are old and your sons do not walk in your ways; now appoint for us a king to govern us like all the nations" (1 Sam. 8:5). This passage apparently reflects the expectations of the autocratic leader style typical of oriental despots. This philosophy sets the stage for the kingship of Saul.

Saul's reign began with promise. He was anointed by Samuel at God's direction (1 Sam. 9:26–10:1), affirmed by signs (10:1-13), chosen with popular acclaim (10:17-24), coronated at Gilgal (11:1-15), wasn't chosen because of the failure of former charismatic leaders (12:1-6), and, consequently, stood in the tradition of the judges (12:7-15). Importantly, Saul masterminded the defeat of the threatening Philistines (14:16-23).

But Saul's kingship was flawed. In fact, 1 Sam. 13:8-15 describes Saul as rejected before his first act as king. Because of Saul's disobedience, Samuel confronted the king: "You have done foolishly; you have not kept the commandment of the Lord your God, . . . now your kingdom shall not continue" (13:13-14a). Stricken by another transgression in his battle against the Amalakites, Saul groveled before Samuel. Saul confessed, "I have sinned; . . . because I feared the people and obeyed their voice" (15:24-25). The leader followed his followers. As a result, the breach between Samuel the prophet and Saul the king was so complete they never saw each other again.

From this point on in Saul's reign, he became increasingly unstable. Young David played his lyre in an effort to calm the mentally disturbed king. Saul liked David and gave him visibility as a military aide. But later Saul became threatened by and jealous of David's military success and set out to kill him. Saul's deepening deterioration was apparent. He was angered by David's triumphs and watched him closely. Saul further responded by ranting, raving, and repeatedly trying to kill David (1 Sam. 18). In the end, Saul feared the Philistines, consulted with the witch of Endor, was wounded and badly defeated by the Philistines, committed suicide, and was finally beheaded and disgraced by his enemies (1 Sam. 28–31).

Saul's story is a tragic one. In the pattern of most Hermits, Saul lost his ability both to influence the nation's goals and to relate well to others.

Who Goes Where?

A myriad of biblical leader types can be explored. Choose a favorite personality from the Bible, and see which leader style your character best fits.

Overview: Biblical Leaders

The four-style leader model can be illustrated by biblical examples. Nehemiah represents Catalyst leaders; the judges, the Commanders; Barnabas, the Encouragers; and King Saul, the Hermits. Other biblical leader personalities can be viewed through the model too.

Review Questions

1. From your own perspective, how many Catalyst, Commander, Encourager, and Hermit leaders can you list from biblical materials?
2. Can you match follower styles and ministry situations (see chapter 4) with the leader style representatives you listed above?

Notes

1. Ernest E. Mosley, "Nehemiah: Builder of Walls and People," in Ernest E. Mosley, ed., *Leadership Profiles from Bible Personalities* (Nashville: Broadman Press, 1979), pp. 62-85.
2. Robert D. Dale, *Ministers as Leaders* (Nashville: Broadman Press, 1984), pp. 128-29.
3. "Reagan as 'Super Leader,' " *Training*, January 1985, p. 14.
4. Robert D. Dale, "Barnabas: Hidden Leader of the New Testament," in Ernest E. Mosley, ed., *Leadership Profiles from Bible Personalities* (Nashville: Broadman Press, 1979), pp. 102-13.

A Selected Bibliography for Biblical Leadership

Dale, Robert D. *Ministers as Leaders*. Nashville: Broadman Press, 1984.

Mosley, Ernest E. ed. *Leadership Profiles from Bible Personalities*. Nashville: Broadman Press, 1979.

Peterson, Eugene H. *Five Smooth Stones for Pastoral Work*. Atlanta: John Knox Press, 1975.

Sanders, J. Oswald. *Spiritual Leadership*. Chicago: Moody Press, 1967.

III.
Solving Leadership Problems:
A Laboratory

— 6 —

DIAGNOSING THE CLIMATE OF YOUR CHURCH

CONGREGATIONS HAVE UNIQUE personalities. They develop climates or atmospheres all their own. While alike in some regards, churches differ in important ways. It's critical, therefore, for church leaders to be able to "read" a congregation and its dynamics. After all, the congregation is the basic organizational unit of ministry. Diagnosing the health (or disease) of the body of Christ is a foundational skill for church leaders who hope to bring healing to their congregations.

Here are two pieces of diagnostic information. First, a description of the diagnostician's role plus a survey of the range of diagnostic tools introduce you to an array of resources for figuring out why your church behaves as it does. Second, a stage-by-stage model of congregational life is described. This "health cycle" can be used to diagnose and help bring vitality to your congregation.

Minister as Sociotherapist

Ministers and other church leaders have to wear many hats. Frequently they provide diagnostic abilities for congregational concerns. That is, they help others figure out what's going on in the larger congregation.

One of the less noticed hats ministry leaders wear is that of sociotherapist.[1] Is that an idea that's familiar to you? Let me describe who sociotherapists are and what they do.

They are therapists—persons who diagnose with an eye toward treating or even healing the group's ailments. They are oriented toward the "socio"—the group and corporate dimensions of congregational life. Sociotherapists focus on the health and care of the congregation as an entity.

A psychiatrist friend of mine left private practice to become the chief executive officer of a medical center. I once asked him how he used his psychiatric training in administration. "It's the same process," he answered. "When I have a management problem to solve, I simply do a differential diagnosis." In other words, he used his medical skills in diagnosis to get a fix on problems, narrow down the range of concerns, zero in on the core of the matter, and apply the most promising cures to the situation. My friend had made a successful transition from psychotherapy to sociotherapy.

Ministers do sociotherapy all the time without using that term when they try to bring a greater degree of health to their congregations. Ministers, like other sociotherapists, use a variety of diagnostic models and perspectives. They bring their experiences, education, and values to the process of creating healthy churches. Often they lean on materials from organizational experts to tell them "six places to look for trouble with or without a theory."[2] This approach is common to the management sciences. But other possibilities are available to ministers too.

Diagnostic Disciplines

Ministers use a full range of disciplines in their congregational diagnostic work. Like most persons who try to solve problems, we characteristically use the disciplines at hand and the tools we're most familiar with. Most of these disciplines deepen our understandings of the history of our congregations.[3]

Sociology provides a common set of implements for exploring congregations. Sociological approaches emphasize the community setting of the congregation, statistical tables, and demographic information. These materials are helpful in enriching your general view of your congregation, especially your view of factors external to the church.

Anthropology also lends some tools to the study of congregations. Ethnographic analysis of a congregation uses observation and interviews to understand the culture of the local church. The findings from this type of research uncover the significance of behaviors, customs, interactions, feelings, and social networks. The internal dynamics of the congregation often are clarified by the ethnographic methods of the anthropologist.

Literary analysis applies the techniques used to understand stories and narratives to diagnosing the congregation. This approach enriches our insights into the flow of corporate life across time. Every congregation has its own unique story. For example, the history of a church is its "plot." Its "setting" is the world view of that church. Its "characterization" is the personality of the congregation, its ethos or pattern of values.

Analysis by Issue

Other organizational experts, using a variety of diagnostic techniques, zero in on single issues within church life. The size, setting, and climate of the congregation are often seen as pivotal interpretation points.

Some congregational experts put considerable stock in the differences *size* makes in the dynamics of local churches. Large and small churches don't operate or feel alike to their members or leaders. Consequently, there's a growing body of literature and studies of congregations by size, particularly the small church.[4]

The *neighborhood setting* of the congregation is also emphasized in some quarters. These consultants specialize in the unique needs and opportunities of rural, rurban (the rural but urbanizing situation), urban, and suburban congregations. Particular attention is paid to congregations in changing settings like the rural-urban fringe or the inner city.[5]

Several resources stress the *atmospheric conditions* of congregations. The "weather" in the church—warm and sunny, cloudy and threatening, stormy and ominous—influences the congregation's actions and reactions. One helpful study distinguishes between ideological and behavioral churches.[6] The ideological church stresses more authoritarian leadership, propositional theology, and indoctrination. The behavioral church, on the other hand, encourages more participative leader styles, relational theology, and Christian service in the congregation and the world. These climates shape the lives of their respective congregations.

Applying the Health Cycle Model

Every minister and church leader has asked, "What's going on in my church? What can I do?" These questions are answered by the "health cycle" model.[7] This approach helps leaders understand the degree of health or disease in their congregation and make sense of the basic behaviors of churches.

In general, a congregation at any point in time is at one of the stages of health or disease depicted below.

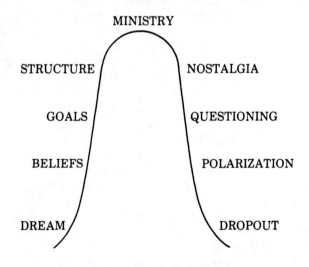

MINISTRY

STRUCTURE   NOSTALGIA

GOALS   QUESTIONING

BELIEFS   POLARIZATION

DREAM   DROPOUT

Illustration 19. Health Cycle Model

Here's an overview of each stage in the health cycle. It may be very helpful to know something about them.

Dream: Focusing Organizational Power

Our dreams, the defining vision of our beings, shape our personal and organizational lives. Remember Willy Loman, the main character in Arthur Miller's *Death of a Salesman*? Willy tried to become a great salesman, failed, and killed himself. After Willy's funeral his sons quietly analyzed the ex-salesman's life. The sons reminisced about Willy's craftsmanship as a carpenter and lamented the fact that Willy hadn't pursued his talent for building things. Instead, he had gone into sales and had lived miserably. Their conclusion? Willy Loman had the wrong dream. Or, more likely, the wrong dream had him. We are known by our personal dreams.

Organizations have their beginnings in their founder's vision. As Emerson put it, organizations are primarily the lengthened shadows of a person. For example, the Bank of America traces its dream and heritage back to its founder, A. P. Giannini. His philosophy in beginning a small bank was simple: every customer deserves a teller. This motto permeated the Bank of America as it grew into a financial giant. The vision of service is a common theme for institutions that last and build a reputation for caring about their clients.

Mutual vision is the foundation for community and organizational health—especially for the health of Christian congregations. A well defined, broadly owned, and sharply focused dream of ministry provides organizational power. From a theological viewpoint, the motivating vision of Jesus was apparently the kingdom of God. Jesus spoke of the kingdom of God (or the kingdom of heaven) more than eighty times in the Gospels. The kingdom was in Jesus' conversations and teachings more often than any other single concern. Jesus' fifty to sixty parables—the core of his teaching and about 35 percent of his recorded instruction—center in "the kingdom of God is like . . ." descriptions and challenges. Basically, the kingdom of

God calls Christians to place their personal and corporate lives under the rule of God. Translated into congregational applications, the kingdom of God provides the fundamental definition for the life and work of the people of God we call the church.

Beliefs: Explaining the Congregational Vision

Congregations give ideas and words to their kingdom dream; we describe those concepts as theology. Our vision of God's kingdom identifies us; our theology explains our convictions and values. In some religious traditions, the corporate expression of their dream of faith is in creeds and covenants. Other religious groups' corporate theology is sung in congregational hymns and spirituals.

My own denominational roots are in the more emotional, informal theological traditions. We noncreedal Baptists sing our faith primarily. I learned this tendency from a college experience. My college roommate and a friend spontaneously started singing through the hymnal one evening. They'd sing, recall how Grandma or some other significant person from their pasts had loved that hymn, spy another friendly hymn, and sing and weep over it. At first I couldn't believe my eyes and ears. Then I saw what was going on. Two fun-loving college boys were expressing their common faith through the words of the hymn writers. They weren't formal theologians, but they believed deeply and could sing their beliefs when someone else supplied the words for them.

Karl Barth, the European theologian and author of many volumes of technical theology, toured the United States some years ago. He was fascinated by a variety of American phenomena, including the spirituals of the black church. In an interview, Barth was asked to state the central facet of his beliefs. He quickly answered, "Jesus loves me this I know, for the Bible tells me so." Barth's summary of his theology was expressed in the words of a simple chorus, a song. I note that children also are usually able to describe their beliefs in music more easily than in structured doctrinal discussions. If this observation is true for your church too, the most important theologian in your congregation may be the person who selects the music for worship and fellowship settings.

The Bible and hymnal are Christianity's two basic books. The Bible records God's revelation of himself to us; the hymnal reflects our response to God's revelation of himself. Both books provide information, inspiration, and tools for undergirding the congregation's unique dream of ministry for itself.

Goals: Turning Dreams into Deeds

Turning "dreams into deeds" is Clarence Jordan's interpretation of Hebrews 11:1. And turning dreams into deeds is exactly what a congregation attempts when it puts its goal-setting process into motion.

In broad terms, churches have two kinds of goals—even if they don't deliberately set goals.[8] Survival and mission goals characterize most congregations. Survival goals usually involve bodies (membership growth), budgets, and buildings. Concentrating on these survival-motivated goals turns congregations inward. Mission goals turn congregations outward and press them to clarify their unique identities, ministry directions, and and community opportunities.

When a congregation is faced with a historical junction, like when a building debt is retired or when a new pastor arrives, the choice between survival and mission is starkly drawn. Faced with goal options, many congregations flee back into survival by erecting a building and incurring new debts with their legal and moral obligations or by ridding themselves of their pastor. Debts force congregations to recruit new members on the basis of their potential offerings; the interim period between pastors often draws a congregation into false unity with an unspoken agreement not to rock the boat—at least until a new pastor arrives. These and other circumstances test a congregation's dream of ministry. Occasionally, congregations discover a tragic fact: survival, not the kingdom of God, is and always has been their only dream.

Structure: Organizing for Action

What you want to do determines how you organize to pursue your goals. As architects know full well, form follows function. Formal structuring or organizing the congregation provides muscle for ministry action and, thereby, strengthens or weakens the church's ability to meet its goals.

Formal organization often is depicted in physical terms, such as a pyramid or a wheel. We're familiar with these organizational images. Remember that formal organization is designed to help congregations reach their official goals.

Congregations also are made up of an invisible type of church—the informal organization. Since not all human needs are easily met by the pursuit of formal organizational goals, an informal organization emerges spontaneously to meet personal needs. The informal organization resembles a network or a web of human interests. For instance, when members feel a need to know that exceeds newsletters, announcements, and bulletin boards, a "grapevine" develops to fill the gap. Likewise, when people feel excluded from the decision-making process, an "underground" emerges. These are natural human needs which call for personal caring and for open congregational organizations. Otherwise, the informal organization can slow or stop church advance.

Wise congregational leaders learn structural skills. (1) They learn to distinguish between the under-organized church (with aspects of its dream unsupported by organizational units) and the over-organized church (with organization units unrelated to its dream). (2) They learn to select the structures which complement their formal goals. (3) They recognize the inevitability of and the legitimate uses of informal organization. (4) They learn to provide leadership for both formal and informal organization.

Ministry: Incarnating the Dream

Ministry is the act of incarnating the kingdom of God in local congregations and communities. From an organizational point of view, ministry depends on a clearly defined and broadly owned kingdom dream, trusting and stable relationships in the congregation, members' needs being met, volunteers being adequately rewarded, high morale in the membership, and a healthy climate in the congregation.

Healthy organizational climates grow out of the norms, or standard operating procedures, of the congregation. Every organization develops a culture of its own with unspoken rules on "how we do things around here." Some norms are positive and growth inducing; others are negative and growth blocking. Norms tend to be invisible but potent forces against change. Confronting norms demands love and timing.

Ministry can proceed indefinitely. But often the accumulation of institutional age, distance from the motivating dream, inclusion of members with diverse expectations, and a succession of pastors with differing perspectives create an organizational plateau. The inertia of the church on the plateau sets in almost imperceptibly, but soon the tilt toward organizational health becomes apparent. Growth, giving, and volunteer participation wane. The seeds of the diseased church are waiting to germinate and sprout any time a congregation loses touch with its dream.

Nostalgia: Wishing for Some Golden Age

Nostalgia raises the "It isn't working as well as it used to, is it?" mood in an organization. This is a cool phase of congregational life when members long for some golden age from the past. Nostalgia tempts us to recover a romanticized memory—usually a selective memory of a time that never existed except in our idealizations. Like newsman Charles Kuralt has observed, there are three kinds of memories—good, bad, and convenient. Nostalgia is mainly the convenient memory.

From a leadership standpoint, nostalgia is uncomfortable. (1) Leaders feel threatened by comparisons with the past. (2) Congregations can be seduced into only looking backward. (3) The most crucial organizational discomfort in nostalgia is potentially devastating: there's little or no loyalty to the present. This posture can freeze a congregation in a damaging or even dooming state of inaction.

Nostalgia is an early warning signal that the slide toward organizational disease is in motion. The alert leader hears the concerns of nostalgic members as a clear indication of the need to dream again.

Questioning: Reaching the Point of No Return

Organizationally speaking, the questioning stage is the point of no return. Either the congregation renews its mission, or its state of disease may deteriorate to a terminal state.

Serious questioning stirs the feelings of uncertainty, irritability, and anger. Tough inquiries about the basic identity of the congregation press leaders. Glib answers don't satisfy. An extended period of questioning may erode its unity and the congregation's ability to hear members' differing concerns.

Polarization: Dividing the House of God

When the disease of the congregation worsens into polarization, conflict erupts and we-they positions are staked out. For many congregations, polarization is a descent into organizational hell, to paraphrase a line from the Apostles' Creed. The escalation of conflict creates a messy situation and lots of right-wrong moralizing.

Our assumptions about conflict determine our strategies for coping with church fights. Consider these perspectives on congregational conflict. (1) Conflict generally indicates a relationship. We rarely waste energy by fussing with strangers. (2) Conflict among friends or acquaintances is especially threatening. After all, the relationship is at stake. And, people who know each other well also know how to cause maximum hurt with minimum effort. (3) When people feel strongly about an issue, their conflicts tend to be heavily emotionally laden. (4) Group conflict produces conflict that polarizes and moralizes. (5) Healthy congregations settle their differences promptly. By dealing with their conflicts more often, they use their ongoing experiences to learn how to resolve their fusses more constructively.(6) Suppressing conflict often leads to explosions. (For additional information on resolving conflicts, see chapter 13.)

Drop Outs: Killing the Dream

When nostalgia deepens, questions remain unanswered, and polarization occurs, apathy is the obvious final step in organizational disease. Members feel alienated from their own church; for some their dream of the kingdom's coming into their lives is no longer seen as possible in this congregational setting. Since some denominations report as many as one-fourth of their members as inactive, the "drop out" phenomenon is a major challenge to local church vitality.

How can the health cycle model be applied to your church to revitalize it? Dream and plan—but that's the theme of the next two chapters.

Overview: Diagnosing Congregational Health

No leader can enhance congregational health without a mental picture of how organizations behave. The health cycle model provides a nine-stage description of the vitality of congregations. This model (and others) gives leaders a useful diagnostic tool and makes them sociotherapists.

Review Questions

1. Can you list and describe the nine stages of the health cycle?
2. Who are sociotherapists?

Notes

1. Edgar H. Schein, *Process Consultation* (Reading, Mass.: Addison-Wesley Publishing Co., 1969).
2. Marvin R. Weisbord, "Organizational Diagnosis: Six Places to Look for Trouble with or Without a Theory," *Group and Organizational Studies* 1, 430-47.
3. For variety of diagnostic methods, see Carl S. Dudley, ed., *Building Effective Ministry* (New York: Harper & Row, 1983), pp. 38-207.
4. Carl S. Dudley, *Making the Small Church Effective* (Nashville: Abingdon Press, 1978) and Lyle E. Schaller, *Looking in the Mirror* (Nashville: Abingdon Press, 1984), pp. 14-37.
5. Lyle E. Schaller, *Hey, That's Our Chuch!* (Nashville: Abingdon Press, 1975).
6. Roger A. Johnson, *Congregations as Nurturing Communities* (Philadelphia: Division of Parish Services, Lutheran Church of America, 1979).
7. Robert D. Dale, *To Dream Again* (Nashville: Broadman Press, 1981). All rights reserved. Used by permission.
8. Donald L. Metz, *New Congregations* (Philadelphia: Westminster Press, 1967).

Selected Bibliography for Congregational Diagnosis

Anderson, James D. *To Come Alive!: Revitalizing the Local Church* (New York: Harper & Row, 1973).

Dale, Robert D. *To Dream Again* (Nashville: Broadman Press, 1981).

French, Wendell L., and Bell, Cecil H., Jr. *Organizational Development: Behavioral Science Interventions for Organization Improvement* (Englewood Cliffs, N.J.: Prentice-Hall, 1978).

Kanter, Rosabeth Moss, and Stein, Barry A., eds. *Life in Organizations: Workplaces as People Experience Them* (New York: Basic Books, 1979).

Kelley, Arleon L. *Your Church: A Dynamic Community* (Philadelphia: Westminster Press, 1982).

Kotter, John P. *Organizational Dynamics: Diagnosis and Intervention* (Reading, Mass.: Addison-Wesley Publishing Co., 1978).

Rosenberg, Seymour L. *Self-Analysis of Your Organization* (New York: AMACOM, 1974).

Schaller, Lyle E. *Hey, That's Our Church!* (Nashville: Abingdon Press, 1975).

Weisbord, Marvin R. *Organizational Diagnosis: A Workbook of Theory and Practice* (Reading, Mass.: Addison-Wesley Publishing Co., 1978).

— 7 —

SHARPENING YOUR CONGREGATION'S VISION

VISION IS THE stuff of the future. The painter Raphael claimed vision was the secret of his artistry: "I just dream dreams and see visions and then I paint around these dreams and visions." Our vision tends to become our reality, the foundation for our actions. Our dreams shape and explain us. Our vision also creates our institutions.

Sharpening your congregation's vision provides it with a foundation for launching its ministries as well as a definition of its future. A clearly stated mission lets us "paint around" our current and projected ministries. At least three aspects of vision contribute to a congregation's dream of ministry: the visions of its individual leaders, a theological ideology, and a congregation-wide process for clarifying and implementing its dream.

In-Visioning: Your Stake in the Kingdom

Your vision of God's kingdom captures you. In-visioning, having a keenly focused dream of the kingdom of God in your life, means you are who you are because of your view of ministry. Keep in mind that the preposition "in" can be used as an intensifier. In-visioning intensifies your dream of God's work in your life and in the world.

What would you do if you read this ad in your daily newspaper? Would you answer it?

WANTED: Dreamers—men and women of all ages and backgrounds, colors, and sizes. To implement vision of a new world. No salary or commission. Long hours and stressful situations. Security marginal now but ultimate later. Resourceful, supportive employer. Apply in person only.

What kind of dreamer are you? Your vision of what God wants from you identifies and motivates your Christian service. It may also influence and shape your congregation's dream too.

Various dreamers have different kinds of vision. Some dreamers are plagued by *myopic vision*. They are so terribly near-sighted that they live only for today. Their vision is fuzzy and is barely focused beyond their noses. They tend to forget the hard-fought lessons of history. Myopic dreamers need to have their vision stretched.

Other dreamers have *peripheral vision*. They see side issues. These visionaries are hampered in moving forward because they catch the threatening images of lurking problems in the corners of their eyes. They don't move ahead for fear that shadowy difficulties will defeat their efforts. These folks are easily distracted.

Some dreamers suffer from *tunnel vision*. They see only what's dead ahead of them and assume that their slender view of reality reflects the whole world. They don't see other persons or issues; they plunge into the narrow future they see and trample on anyone who wanders into their paths.

The healthiest dreamers have *panoramic vision*. They see the big picture. They live for more than the here and now (unlike those with myopic vision.) They see what's ahead of them (unlike persons with only peripheral vision) as well as what's to the sides (unlike the folks with tunnel vision). These generalist thinkers are who most church members are referring to when they say, "We need leaders with vision."

Visions. Dreams. Prophetic words and deeds. They build

our futures. Dreams can upset those who have either no ideas about the future or are tied to the past. Remember Joseph's visionary tendencies and their results? Genesis 37:5 reminds us that "Joseph had a dream, and when he told it to his brothers they only hated him the more." Clear dreams energize dreamers—and sometimes their opponents too.

Visioning: A Theology for Ministry

Vision is the power you have to see, imagine, and perceive things not yet visible and events not yet attempted. Church leaders and congregations need a basic theological stance for their visions in order to launch and implement effective ministry.

Fundamental to the ministry of Jesus was the kingdom of God, or what Clarence Jordan called the "God movement." The kingdom dream had captured Jesus. He spoke of it more than any other theme. Jesus lived (and died) for the God movement. If we choose Jesus as our ministry model, the kingdom of God must be prominent in our lives. All else is secondary and next best.

The kingdom of God describes a spiritual commonwealth embracing all who do the Father's will. The God movement calls us into a dynamic reign, not a static rule. God, in his sovereign activity, dares us, stretches us, surprises us, and keeps us dreaming.

The broad contours of theology in the kingdom dream remind us of several bedrock themes.[1] (1) God's reigning in individuals and over their organizations is the kingdom in action. The enacted kingdom demonstrates God's sovereign work in redeeming persons and in establishing a new human order. (2) The king of Jesus' kingdom is a father. That's the primary paradox of the God movement. (3) The kingdom builds toward a community we call the church. (4) Jesus himself defines the kingdom. (5) Citizens of the kingdom adopt a new lifestyle. Christians express love in practical acts.

Churches and other Christian organizations are usually born out of the burning convictions of men and women about what God wants them to do here and now. These convictions, reduced into an easy-to-remember slogan, represent a profound statement of values. These values define their reason for being. The challenge, then, is to structure ministry around a basic value and to publicize the mission for all to know and follow.

Envisioning: Congregational Dreaming

A defined congregational dream sets the stage for the health cycle's sequence. Here's a quick review of the model described in detail in the preceding chapter.

- A dream gives birth to a congregation.
- Beliefs provide a doctrinal agreement for congregational action.
- Church goals extend the congregation's shared dream and beliefs.
- Structure organizes the congregation for pursuing its goals and advancing its dream.
- Ministry shows the congregation reaching out to others, developing its members, and living out its dream in Christian love.
- Nostalgia reflects a wistful longing for a comfortable past—real or imagined.
- Questioning marks the point of no return for the congregation, organizationally speaking. Either the church redefines and is revitalized by its dream, or its rate of decline speeds its slide into disease.
- Polarization creates an organizational climate in which church members mistake one another for the enemy and fall into conflict.
- Dropouts result when the dream of effective ministry in this place dies and members retreat into inactivity.

A step-by-step process can assist congregations in defining and sharing their kingdom dream. This process is designed to help church leaders involve members in building consensus about the congregation's mission and in gaining ownership for the ministries growing out of the group's dream.

Step One: How Can the Congregation Be Effectively Involved in the Dreaming Process?

Dreaming calls for broad involvement on the part of the membership. A "town meeting" approach to gathering information and reaching consensus opens the process to maximum participation. Although this philosophy slows down the pace of the process, congregation–wide participation builds ownership in advance for implementing the dream.

While there are an almost infinite number of approaches to awakening a congregational dream, here's the process one church used.[2] The time frame involved in the process described below was from March to December.

1. The pastor wrote a series of newsletter articles to whet members' appetites for the dreaming process. The pastor had already discovered that a large number of members were motivated to minister more aggressively but were unclear on what to do.
2. The church elected a New Dream Committee. The eleven-member committee represented a cross section of the congregation. Together they studied the health cycle model discussed in the previous chapter. Then they spent the summer surveying the needs of the church and community. Next, they used the church's midweek family night dinners to present and hear reactions to their primary research findings.
3. The pastor preached a sermon series on dreaming.
4. The congregation used several resource persons to raise consciousness and train members.

5. Lay leaders gave their perspectives publicly during several morning worship services.
6. A survey gathered information on how much effort members were willing to invest in implementing the emerging dream. Specific changes, sacrifices, and assignments were tested by this process.
7. The New Dream Committee hosted a hearing. The entire congregation was asked to give feedback to a range of possible recommendations. At the conclusion of the hearing the congregation rank ordered their preferred elements of the developing mission statement.
8. A formal presentation was made of the new dream and the recommendations growing out of it. A congregational vote ratified the new dream and its implemenation.
9. Throughout the dreaming process, all the congregation's channels for communication—newsletters, presentations in a variety of congregational meetings, bulletin boards, and the like—were used to publicize and clarify possibilities.
10. A service of commitment symbolized the covenant to support the new dream of the congregation.

In less than two years twenty-five of the twenty-six original initiatives were successfully completed. What accounts for the momentum this church experienced in implementing this portion of its long-term dream? The members saw the dreaming process as theirs; they took ownership of the product. The leaders guided the dreaming process without controlling it.

Whatever the details of the process, a feedback loop should be developed to cycle and recycle information during the dreaming process.

• Generate a draft statement of the congregation's dream for ministry.
• Study the opportunities in and barriers to the congregation's dream.

● Help the leadership team propose an outline of the dream to the congregation.
● Listen to the congregation's response and probe their statements to be sure they are heard and understood.
● Assist the leader team in considering the feedback they've received from the congregation at large.
● Take a reformed dream statement back to the congregation for their reaction.
● Repeat this cycle of actions until the leadership team and the congregation are thinking of ministry in the same concepts.
● Get a formal adoption of the dream statement when a consensus emerges.

Step Two: What Is Our Basic Purpose?

A mission statement describes why the congregation exists and what it will attempt to contribute to the God movement. This precise and concise affirmation tells the church what its target is. That's what a dream does; it points out the bull's-eye.

Look at these sample mission statements:

● Old First exists to tell non-Christians about Christ and to develop believers in faith.
● Our seminary's purpose is to train men and women for the full range of Christian ministries.
● This mission board will establish new congregations for witnessing and ministering and will enable churches and denominational groups to open new frontiers in sharing the gospel of Jesus Christ.

"We've always done it this way" or "All churches do this" aren't necessarily reasons enough for existing. These generalized slogans don't make decent mission statements. Effective churches know exactly what they're trying to do. Their mission statements balance out the congregation's need for flexibility with their need for stability.

Basically, a mission statement puts the congregation's dream into words and ideas that can be communicated to members and prospective members. (1) Mission statements explain us to ourselves. (2) Mission statements also explain us to outsiders. Beyond this specific result, mission statements have several other functions.

• Mission statements mark our organizational boundaries and differentiate what we will do and what we won't (or can't) do.
• Mission statements describe the needs in our community and our congregation that we will try to meet.
• Mission statements also describe how we will try to respond to the needs we've targeted.
• Mission statements provide a foundation for planning.

Writing out your dream statement is a creative and exacting process. Try this. Complete three unfinished sentences by writing a brief paragraph in response to each sentence.

First, complete this sentence: Our congregation's basic reason for existing is . . . . Write down as many basic dream statements for your church as you can think of. To stretch imaginations pose these questions. What's our congregation's fundamental purpose? What justifies our congregation's existence? Or, to press the point further, use this inquiry: If our church were to disappear, what would be lost to God's kingdom? Note any priorities that emerge from your response.

Second, finish this sentence: Because of our congregation's dream, we will minister by. . . . Ask these clarifying questions. What bedrock, essential ministry actions are implied by our congregation's vision of itself? What are we compelled to do by Christian concern? What spiritual breach of contract will be committed if we don't act now? Watch for priorities to clarify themselves further in this step.

Third, write your response to this sentence: The special people we will minister to are. . . . Note any target audiences, specific constituent groups, geographic limits, and time sequences implied by your statements.

Try to condense each paragraph to one clear sentence. These sentences should yield a working dream statement for others to consider and respond to.

Step Three: What Are the Unique Resources of Our Congregation?

Congregations have several key resources—people, money, buildings, information, and vision. The mix of these internal assets gives the congregation its special identity and extraordinary possibilities for ministry.

Step Four: What Are the Unusual Needs of Our Constituency?

The needs of the community uncover some ministry opportunities beyond the congregation. Census data and municipal planning information round out the impressionistic material church members may have already (see chapter 8). These concerns are mostly external to the congregation. Additionally, the congregation's internal needs also call for a faith response.

Step Five: How Can We Focus Our Dreams?

The power and motivational energy of the kingdom dream provide a launching pad for quality ministry. Since the majority of Jesus' parables begin with "the kingdom of God is like . . . ," preaching and teaching on the parables will help church members examine material for stating their dream. Looking at the images and themes of the kingdom in the Gospels brings greater focus on congregational explorations regarding their dream.

Another approach to help clarify congregational dreams involves studying the rich variety of images of the church in the New Testament. Understanding what the Bible says about the emerging church helps us define the dream of our church. For example, Paul S. Minear has identified 722 New Testament passages in which varied images of the church are described.[3]

body of Christ (1 Cor. 12:27)
chosen people (1 Pet. 2:10)
people of God (Heb. 8:10)
people of light (1 Thess. 5:5)
priesthood of believers (1 Pet. 2:9)
salt of the earth (Matt. 5:13)
stewards (1 Pet. 4:10)
temple of the living God (2 Cor. 6:16)

One minister friend uses "pastoral letters" to keep the congregation's vision sharply focused. These occasional letters are aimed at specific issues in the church's life and are intended to call the congregation to action around a narrowly stated theme.

Step Six: How Do We Anticipate Making Our Ministry Dream Come True?

Planning helps congregations think in an anticipatory mode, lessening the possibility of falling into a reactive stance. Proactive rather than reactive behaviors put congregations on the offensive. Planning congregations exercise initiative. Like boxers who jab and move forward instead of retreating and counterpunching, planning chooses a preferred future and acts to claim that future.

Since all planning is abstract (dealing with an uncertain future), an increasing number of congregations are using project-oriented planning approaches. Projects have the advantage of being concrete, tangible ministry events. Ministry projects represent a strategic choice. They are slices of a longer-range view. A project is a sliver of the congregation's dream. After the mission statement has defined the direction of the church's dream, then ministry projects become stepping stones to reach the long-term target of ministry. (For additional information on planning for change, see chapter 8.)

Overview: Building a Congregation's Vision

A vision acts like a magnet, drawing a congregation along toward its future in ministry. Three ingredients contribute to a keenly focused ministry dream: the personal visions of leaders, a theology or ideology for ministry, and a congregational process for defining the group's vision. A ministry vision provides a foundation for planning.

Review Questions

1. What's your personal vision of ministry? Why is it important?
2. What's your theology or ideology for ministry?
3. What are the steps in a process for helping congregations define and share their ministry dreams?

Notes

1. A. M. Hunter, *Jesus: Lord and Saviour* (Grand Rapids: Wm. B. Eerdmans Publishing Co., 1976), pp. 47-57.
2. Timothy K. Norman, "The Process of Leading Ginter Park Baptist Church to Develop a Church Growth Dream," (unpublished D. Min. project report, Southeastern Baptist Theological Seminary, 1983).
3. Paul S. Minear, *Images of the Church in the New Testament* (Philadelphia: Westminster Press, 1970).

Selected Bibliography for Sharpening Congregational Vision

Anderson, John D. *To Come Alive!: Revitalizing the Local Church.* New York: Harper & Row, 1973.

Callahan, Kennon L. *Twelve Keys to an Effective Church.* New York: Harper & Row, 1983.

Deal, Terrence E., and Kennedy, Allan A. *Corporate Cultures.* Reading, Mass.: Addison-Wesley Publishing Co., 1982.

Elder, Lloyd. *Blueprints.* Nashville: Broadman Press, 1984.

Kelley, Arleon L. *Your Church: A Dynamic Community.* Philadelphia: Westminster Press, 1982.

Peters, Thomas J., and Waterman, Robert H., Jr. *In Search of Excellence: Lessons from America's Best-Run Companies.* New York: Harper & Row, 1982.

— 8 —

PLANNING FOR CHANGE

RECENTLY I SAW a poster that caught my eye and imagination. Its message was simple. "Plan ahead. It wasn't raining when Noah built the ark." Planning helps church leaders live out the truth of British author Samuel Johnson's dictum: "The future is purchased by the present." Change management is a basic leadership opportunity. Planning allows us to turn today into a better tomorrow.

Leader as Change Agent

Ministers help their members and congregations manage change. After all, change is inevitable. Consequently, living effectively and happily calls on us to deal well with transitions.

Different leaders, because of their distinctive leader styles, use a variety of change strategies, assume different roles, adopt a range of planning models,[1] and create distinctive congregational moods. Let's overview the possibilities available to ministers as they try to guide change processes (review the leader style options in chapter 3).

Catalysts and Change Agentry

Catalysts use participative decision-making as their basic philosophy of managing change. They know people support the changes they help plan. In other words, Catalysts recognize that all who will be expected to implement a decision deserve to be included in making that decision. Participative strategies build for long-range change by enhancing the congregation's spirit and by maximizing the planning resources of its members. To implement this participative philosophy, Catalysts utilize a variety of roles: designer and manager of change processes, identifier of options, and adviser-resource person.

Catalysts tend to use an affirm-and-build planning approach. This model raises several key questions as its planning framework. (1) What are the unique strengths, assets, and resources we can affirm about our congregation? As the distinctive resources of the congregation are identified, ways these assets can be used to reinforce, expand, and extend the basic ministries of the congregation can be listed. Most congregations will discover a dozen or so strengths they can take ownership of for their future ministry planning. Beginning with the distinctive resources of the church provides a positive foundation for building a change management plan. (2) What are the ministry vacuums and unmet religious needs of un-churched persons in our community? (3) How can we use our congregational resources to minister to our un-churched neighbors? (4) How can we create a new, representative planning task force to turn our ministry dream into practice? (5) How can we develop and adopt a plan of ministry we can implement and evaluate? The affirm-and-build model fosters an optimistic mood in the congregation. Members take a "With God's help, we can do it!" attitude about the future.

Commanders and Change Agentry

Commanders push for productivity. They want re-sults—now! Commanders press for more efficiency and organizational momentum. To achieve their goals, Commanders assume a range of roles: goal selector, advocate-salesperson, and director of change processes.

Commanders tend to adopt a church-community planning model with a narrowed agenda. This approach focuses on congregational survival and members' needs more than general ministry and outreach. Church-community planning models frequently emphasize buildings and properties. The congregational mood the Commander's approach promotes is "Which battles should we fight today?"

Encouragers and Change Agentry

Encouragers try to enrich congregations' atmospheres. They concentrate on fellowship and members' morale. In order to facilitate this goal, Encouragers fill several relationally oriented roles: feedback giver, cheerleader, and mediator.

Encouragers assume a life-cycle model for planning. They see congregations moving through a natural cycle from birth to growth to maturity to decline to death, as individuals do. While the logic of this approach is obvious, the life-cycle approach can take on a note of fatalism. Members may assume "Our congregation's situation is a natural phenomenon and may get worse before it gets better."

Hermits and Change Agentry

Hermits react to outside pressure more than they deliberately attempt to manage change. When other congregational leaders insist that new ministries are required or when they feel neighboring congregations have seized the ministry initiative in the community, Hermits feel pressured to do something. They assume the roles of reluctant assistant, reflector, or spectator.

Hermits usually use a problem-solving approach for planning. This model lists all the problems the congregation needs to cope with. Unfortunately, problems multiply. Centering on problems has a way of creating a negative climate that opens the door to blaming, scapegoating, and the search for simplistic or escapist solutions. In the end, the congregation may feel overwhelmed by the combination of a myriad of problems and a shortage of leadership. "We give up," they admit as they raise their white flags of surrender.

Ministry leaders don't have an option about serving as change agents. Change management goes with the territory when leadership is assumed. But change agents do have a choice of the strategies, roles, and models they use, and, therefore, the congregational moods they create by their planning efforts. Leaders can choose how they will plan. But they must plan.

Why Plan?

Planning takes a congregation's dream, or image of the future, and tries to write history in advance. Plans written and adopted by the congregation at large become dynamite for leaders. Such plans provide the organization its tools for creating its destiny or at least adapting to its future. Plans stretch us. The famed American architect Frank Lloyd Wright advised, "Make no little plans for there is no magic in them to stir people's souls."

Effective plans give congregations four valuable assets.

● Goal ownership—Group goals build public commitment for implementation.
● Ministry continuity—Ministry programs and projects are synchronized by the long-range and short-term goals of the group.
● Flexible options—Even the best of plans can go awry. However, the planning process generates other possibilities which provide a Plan B to fall back on.
● Precise direction—Plans select specific targets. The purpose of the congregation is kept clearly defined and

publicly understood. The congregation's decisions are openly made.

Decisions: The Bricks and Mortar of Planning

Decisions form the baseline of planning. The decisions we make provide the raw materials for our planning efforts. The following decision-making cycle may be used over and over as we generate the stuff for planning.

- Gather and analyze the available information.
- Predict the likely outcomes.
- Evaluate your projected outcomes.
- Create and compare all available options.
- Select the best alternative from the available options.
- Define and detail your plans.
- Act on your plans.
- Measure results.
- Re-evaluate your plan and collect new information.
- Decide again and plan again.

Making decisions grows out of the mix of the situation's controllables and the relevant uncontrollables. Take a Sunday school growth campaign as an example of dealing with the controllables and uncontrollables of planning. The controllable factors include gathering study materials, training teachers, and cultivating prospective Sunday school members. An uncontrollable factor might be a blizzard on high attendance day. Planning's outcomes emerge from the controllable-uncontrollable mixture.

Types of Planning

Other than the leader's attempt at personal planning, there are at least three basic types of congregational planning: directional, annual, and operational planning. The distinctions between planning types are both *when,* or the length of time involved, and *what,* the nature of the events planned for.

Directional, or long-range planning, tries to forecast the congregation's future from one to ten years in advance. In directional planning, the "planning horizon," or the length of time your plan projects itself into the future, is extended one to ten years into the future. Two rules guide how time horizons are used in long-range planning. (1) Plan as far ahead as reasonable accuracy allows. (2) The farther into the future you extend your planning horizon, the more tentative your predictive plans become. In highly fluid congregations or in mobile communities with rapidly changing needs, the time dimension shortens and may even require multiple planning tracks.

Annual planning calls for discovering and structuring the basic actions needed to sustain the congregation's movement and momentum toward its more immediate dream. These purposeful actions usually are limited to one year or less.

Operational planning breaks approaching events or projects down into components; it details the steps required as well as the persons responsible for using resources. Operational planning uses time horizons of months, weeks, days, and possibly hours. The more the time horizon shortens, the more detailed planning becomes.

Whichever type of planning is appropriate to the task, a structured process will guide planners. Note the steps below.

The Planning Process

The planning process requires a congregation to answer at least seven questions. These inquiries are repeated every time the congregation attempts to plan.

● *"Who are we?"* Defining a congregation's basic identity, or dream, is the most fundamental step leaders take. The foundational vision of the congregation spotlights the driving force of the group. Management theorist Peter Drucker claims that "What business are we in?" is the bottom-line question effective organizations answer constantly and keep clear.[2]

• *"Where are we?"* This query causes congregations to check where they are in their use of recources and in seizing their opportunities. "Where are we?" reminds leaders that organizations have continuity in history—a past, a present, and a future.

• *"Where do we want to go?"* Congregations can, to a large extent, select their preferred futures. Choosing ministry targets determines in which directions the organization will proceed.

• *"How are we going to get there?"* Projects, ministry programs, and tactics provide the nuts and bolts of planning. These actions guide the implementation process.

• *"When will we get there?"* No plan is complete until the goals are dated. Good goals are measured in terms of timing, quantity, and quality.

• *"How much of our resources will we expend?"* Institutions have to use their resources carefully—members, properties, tithes and offerings, and information. How much of each kind of resource will be committed to the pursuit of ministry goals is a necessary planning question.

• *"How will we know we've successfully implemented our plan?"* Evaluation completes the planning cycle and kicks off a new planning process. Evaluation requires that congregations measure their performance against their purpose. Evaluation involves both planners and implementers, inquires of both activists and those who chose not to take part, asks for both positive and negative impressions and facts, and uses both qualitative and quantitative feedback sources.

Information Resources for Congregational Planning

Most congregational planning groups have ready access to information from within their own local church. However, external resources are crucial too. Effective planning is facilitated by (1) a planning workbook, such as, Edward R. Dayton's *God's Purpose/Man's Purpose.*[3] and (2) an array of factual information from national, regional, and local sources. Scan the checklist below for available sources of relevant information.

National Sources

Ask your denominational headquarters for planning guides, statistical studies, and programming information. Also, write to the Superintendent of Documents, Washington, DC 20025, for a list of publications based on data from the latest national census.

Regional Sources

Highway department
Map of buildings and roads in county
Data on contemplated changes in highways or traffic patterns

Agricultural extension agent
Maps of districts in county
Changes since last census in tenancy, economic class of farms, numbers of farms and farmers, off-farm work
Organizations in church communities
Community improvement programs
Attitudes of residents, leadership potential

Home demonstration agent
Organizations in church communities
Community improvement programs
Attitudes of residents, leadership potential

Superintendent of schools
School district lines, present and contemplated changes
School census or average daily attendance for U.S. census year and present year (or enrollment at a given date in census year and same date in present year)
Extra-curricular activities in schools

111

Plans for new schools or new buildings
Studies of population change since census, or more detailed analysis than in census

Public health officer
Studies of mental and physical health needs of area
Vital statistics (births and deaths since census)
Estimates and projections of population

Public welfare officer
Studies of social problems of area
Comparison of community being studied with itself over a period of time, or with others

County sheriff or county court
Studies of justice needs of area
Delinquency rate

Planning commission
Studies of metropolitan areas in the region
Trends in nonfarm industry and residence
Maps of region
Master plan for regional development

Associations of churches/denominational agencies
Studies of religious needs
Data on size and program of churches and projected activities

Local Sources

Planning commission or zoning board
City map
Land use data
Zoning map and/or data
Street and highway plans
Population studies (density and projected density, projected total)
Map or building permit data

Building inspector or city engineer
Availability of sewerage and water facilities

Trends in residential development (building permits issued for new homes)

Utility research department (telephone, electricity, water)
Studies made of development patterns
Trends in residential development

Real estate board
Studies made of building trends
Trends in industrial and residential development

Chamber of commerce
Trends in industrial and residential development
Reference to other planning sources

Public library
Studies of area
U.S. census publication (in large cities)

Superintendent of schools
(See regional section)

Council of social agencies, community chest
Studies of human needs of area
Community needs

Public health officer
Studies of area (in one city, record of building and demolition by census tracts)
(See regional section)

Public welfare officer
(See regional section)

City court
(See regional section)

Recreation commission
Studies of recreation needs of area

Council of churches, research and planning staff
Studies of area (data on size and program of churches)

Projected activities of denominations
House-to-house census reports or data
Yearbooks of denominations
Possible coordination in current or future studies

Other Area Research Sources

Community college, college, or university department of
    business and public administration, business re-
    search, sociology, planning, or demographics
File of area studies made
Possible coordination in current or future studies
Reference to other pertinent data

Theological seminary/Christian college
    File of religious studies made
    Library file of other pertinent religious data
    Possible coordination in current or future studies

Planning and Implementing: Two Sides of the Same Coin

Congregations plan from ends to means and implement
their plans from means to ends. Ends provide the planning
target to shoot at; means lend tracks to run on. Ends tell
what the congregation will attempt; means describe *how*
planning moves from targets to tracks, from where we
want to be to where we are. Implementation moves along
tracks toward targets, from where we are to where we
want to be. In short, planning and implementing those
plans are simply two sides of the same coin.

Overview: Planning Change

Leading change processes is a basic ministry. Different
leaders take varied approaches to planning—whether

they are doing directional (long-range), annual, or operational (detail) planning. A simple planning process asks: Who are we? Where are we? Where do we want to go? How are we going to get there? When will we get there? How much of our resources will we expend? and How will we know we've successfully implemented our plan?

Review Questions

1. Can you match leader styles with planning models?
2. Can you identify three basic types of planning?
3. Can you list the key questions in the planning process?

Notes

1. Lyle E. Schaller and Charles A. Tidwell, *Creative Church Administration* (Nashville: Abingdon Press, 1975), pp. 55-65.
2. Peter Drucker, *Management: Tasks, Responsibilities, Practices* (New York: Harper & Row, 1974), pp.74-94.
3. Edward R. Dayton, *God's Purpose/Man's Purpose: A Workbook* (Monrovia, Calif.: World Vision International, 1974).

Selected Bibliography on Planning for Change

Dayton, Edward R. *God's Purpose/Man's Purpose: A Workbook.* Monrovia, Calif.: World Vision International, 1974.

Ellis, Daryl J., and Pekar, Peter P., Jr. *Planning for Nonplanners.* New York: Amacom, 1980.

Schaller, Lyle E., and Tidwell, Charles A. *Creative Church Administration.* Nashville: Abingdon Press, 1975.

Tucker, Grayson L., Jr. *A Church Planning Questionnaire.* Self published, 1982.

CHAPTER

— 9 —

BUDGETING FOR MINISTRY ACTION

CONGREGATIONS HAVE TOO often followed the haphazard "Let's take last year's numbers and add inflation" formula for budgeting. That approach ensures that flaws in the church's ministry programs are perpetuated and magnified. Effective leaders have found a better way—ministry action budgeting.

Views of Budgeting

Budgeting in congregations can be viewed from a range of perspectives. For example, a church budget can be examined theologically, practically, and congregationally.

Theologically, a church's budget is a theological document. A budget reveals the congregation's dream. According to Lyle Schaller, a church budget "identifies the gods that are worshiped in that organization, the ranking of those gods in that organization's hierarchy."[1] Values (both personally and congregationally) are reflected in how money is spent.

Practically, congregational budgeting is planned resources management. A budget plans the coordinated use of the congregation's primary resources:

money through the adopted budget;
time through a ministry calendar;
facilities through the development and maintenance of

116

buildings and physical properties; and
people through a plan for evangelism, Christian
development, and leadership enlistment and
training.

Congregationally viewed, budgeting gives an opportunity to broaden the participation base for ministry. Too many congregations reflect the 80/20 rule—80 percent of the ministry is done and 80 percent of the money is given by only about 20 percent of the membership.

Budgeting Principles

Three affirmations provide a foundation for budgeting congregations. Wise leaders will build on these guidelines.

● Planning precedes budgeting. Without a planning process, the budgeting process is aimless. Leaders plan well in order to budget effectively.
● Dreams are translated into dollars by budgets. The congregation's vision of the kingdom of God becomes operational in ministry and budgeting.
● Stewardship is larger than money. Stewardship permeates all of life; budgeting focuses primarily on ministry and money. A perspective on stewardship provides a broad base for the narrower concerns of budgeting.

Stewardship and Budgeting

Stewardship is our response to God as creator.[2] God has allowed human beings to become his junior partners and trustees in creation. A stewardship pattern is made apparent in the order of creation. Note the principles below.

Things are to be used responsibly. The natural level of creation is for human care and consumption. The land, woods, water, and air are ours to be tended and expended with Christian concern.

117

People are to be loved responsibly. The human level of creation is intended for neighborly love and care. The horizontal dimension of creation calls us to "love your neighbor as yourself " (Matt. 22:39).

God is to be worshiped. We revere and give allegiance to the Creator. We recognize that the vertical relationship of God with us human beings redeems all other relationships. Only God deserves our awe and ultimate commitment.

The challenge of Christian stewardship is to *use* things, *love* persons, and *worship* God without mixing up the verbs and the objects. It's sinful, for instance, to use God or love things or worship people. I overheard a troubling conversation in a restaurant in Ada, Oklahoma. One waitress said to another, "The tips are better when I read my Bible and pray before I come to work." At first I was impressed by the woman's piety. Then, as I heard her continue to talk, I became uncomfortably suspicious that her reason for praying was to manipulate God magically into blessing her. If that was her intent, she had become an irresponsible steward.

Stewardship lends a foundation for designing congregational budgets. In one sense, a healthy view of stewardship provides a launching pad to a wholesome approach to ministry and budgeting.

How Budgets Have Been Constructed

Historically, several approaches to budgeting have been used. Years ago some churches charged dues and conscripted funds from their members. Other churches rented their pews. In some cases, Sunday school classes developed budgets separate from the larger congregation. More recently, a unified budgeting approach has generally standardized having one coordinated budget for the entire congregation.

Two styles of unified budgeting have emerged. *Line item budgeting* lists items and matches those lines with dollar amounts. This format calls attention to totals expended rather than to ministry performed. For example, in many smaller congregations, one-half to two-thirds of the overall church budget goes to the pastor's salary and upkeep. When such a noticeable proportion of the budget goes to only one line item, some members may interpret: "Most of our money is given to the pastor. Let him do the work." *Ministry action budgeting,* the second style of unified budgeting, is gaining popularity and is the approach this book prefers.[3]

Ministry action budgeting builds on the zero base budgeting theory. That is, every budget account is wiped clean every year, and all expenses are justified every year according to whether or not projected expenses can be demonstrated to advance the mission of the organization. Each organizational unit begins without any funding, proposes its activities for the next year, costs out every proposed ministry action, and then prioritizes each of its decision packages for committee and congregational consideration.

Zero base budgeting approaches contain both advantages and disadvantages. First, let's look at the plus side. (1) A congregational plan of priorities, or a dream, is the basic beginning point. (2) Every program of ministry receives a thorough, annual evaluation. (3) Money can, therefore, be directed toward priorities. (4) Waste can often be located and eliminated so money is saved. On the other hand, let's consider the minus side now. (1) This approach is relatively new. Traditionalized congregations may prefer to continue doing budgeting their usual way without examination. (2) Some people experience a budget cut as psychological rejection. That is, if your budget is cut, you may feel like someone has cut your throat. (3) Occasionally, a job (and, therefore, an employee) is deleted. Many congregations aren't comfortable with supervising or disciplining their employees, much less eliminating them.

Ministry action budgeting in churches suggests several

special adaptations. (1) The zero base style of budgeting applies primarily to program expenses. Debts and fixed costs remain constant as moral and legal obligations. (2) Church program organizations are caused to evaluate their ministry efforts by their contributions to the congregation's dream. (3) Planning and ministry groups are caused to find and cut out their worse spent dollars and, by their own prioritizing, place their least important program actions in jeopardy.

The process described below develops the ministry action budgeting approach. Notice how crucial dreaming and planning are to launching a ministry action budgeting process.

A Budgeting Process

Budgeting is a pivotal leadership process. Why? Because budgeting expresses your congregation's dream in dollars. Budgets build on plans and spotlight a priority slice of your congregation's vision for immediate implementation. Note the step-by-step process below for leadership actions that are integral to budgeting. This process usually takes from ten to twelve weeks to implement.

• *Lead your ministry staff—laity and clergy—to evaluate the congregation's ministries.* Ongoing processes generally begin and end with evaluation. Periodically, therefore, congregational leaders need to pause and deliberately check on the progress of ministries and programs. Leaders can ask: How much progress have we made? Are we on course with our goals? Are we on time and keeping pace with our deadlines? Do we need to change course? How can we become more efficient and effective? Which new opportunities and needs do we need to attend to now? Do we have ministries we need to drop?

• *Lead your leadership corps to present potential ministry action proposals.* Several formal church actions are appropriate at this stage. If a budget committee hasn't been selected by the congregation, that action is now timely. Then the budget committee reviews long-range plans and ministries in process in order to isolate key needs of the congregation and community. With this backlog of information, the budget committee can now invite all the program groups and any church committee that uses funds to submit ministry action proposals.

Ministry action propoals are written descriptions of projected Christian acts that will help the congregation love and evangelize its world and nurture and train its members. Only organizational groups are invited to suggest ministry actions that tap congregational funds. (This guideline is intended to reduce the possibility that independent actions by individual members can claim church monies for private projects.) The sample proposal form on the next page offers one format for triggering the budgeting proposal.

At this point the process narrows a bit so the budget committee can develop the budget document itself.

• *Lead your budget committee to analyze the proposed ministry actions.* The congregation's dream becomes the yardstick for evaluating budget requests with their specified ministry actions. Each proposal must demonstrate its contribution to the dream of the congregation. The crucial question becomes, Will this ministry action help the congregation live out its vision concretely? Additional inquiries aid in clarifying the practicality of the submitted proposals. Does this ministry action support congregational priorities and goals? Is this proposal linked to a productive program? Does this ministry action proposal represent the best way to extend this portion of the congregation's dream? Is the expense of this proposed ministry action in proportion to available funds?

The budget committee now prioritizes all the ministry action proposals in relation to the congregation's basic vision. These rankings of projects—essential, important but not essential, or good but less important—help the

A Budgeting Proposal for Ministry Action

Project or Ministry: _____

_____

_____

_____

Responsible Church Organization: _____

_____

_____

_____

The ministry we intend to do is . . .

This ministry will undergird (or has undergirded) the
   congregation's dream by . . .

This ministry is needed because . . .

The detailed financial breakdown and total cost of
   this ministry action are . . .

In two years, this ministry action will allow our
   congregation to _____

At a projected cost of _____

In five years? _____

At what cost? _____

In order to judge this proposal, consider these back-up
options. (1) If this project can't be funded as proposed, our
best alternative (actions and costs) is . . .

(2) Another possible alternative (actions and costs) is . . .

Illustration 20. Ministry Action Budgeting Proposal

committee determine how to allocate the congregation's funds.

• *Lead your budget committee to design a budget document that aligns the dollars with the dream of the congregation.* The budget format should reflect the high priority aspects of the congregation's dream in categories—missions and outreach ministries, pastoral ministries, Christian education ministries, worship ministries, social ministries, ministry support and administration, and facilities ministries. (Personnel costs should be placed in the budget under the appropriate ministry category rather than in a separate staff section.) Line items are replaced by key ministry actions; the dream, therefore, is given more visibility than mere dollars.

• *Lead your budget committee to present the budget document to the congregation at large.* The ministries of the congregation are now presented for review. In this format the dollars will be secondary to the dream. Members see clearly, for instance, what education or outreach is and does, not what it costs. Ideally, a discussion forum separate from decision-making pressures can be provided. Feedback from the membership regarding the budget should be taken seriously. With any necessary adjustments incorporated, the final budget should be formally adopted by the congregation.

• *Lead your members to underwrite the budget.* The promotion and pledging of the budget now remains. A variety of approaches is available. Use the approach that your congregation is comfortable with. As a rule, more personal presentations generally get the best responses from congregational members.

• *Lead your treasurer to report on ministry progress rather than only on income and expenditures.* Personalized reports using testimonies, audiovisuals, and selected success stories graphically show how the congregation is implementing its dream in the world. These progress reports depict ministries performed instead of dollars coming in and going out of church bank accounts.

• *Lead your congregational leaders to review ministries annually.* Now the process has come full cycle. At this stage it's timely to evaluate how the ministry actions have contributed to progress toward the congregation's dream.

Guidelines for Budgeting Leaders

Several principles can guide congregational budgeting leaders. These ideas provide a checklist for budgeting.

• Dreaming and planning lend a foundation for budgeting and budgeting processes.
• Budgeting expresses the congregation's values.
• Comprehensive and unified budgeting approaches reduce the need for special offerings outside the budget plan and discourage piecemeal planning and financing.
• Budgeting committees should be representative of the congregation at large.
• Budget committees deserve orientation and training.
• Budgets reflect people programs and ministry commitments more than mere dollars.

Overview: Ministry Action Budgeting

Ministry action budgeting builds on the foundation of a clear congregational vision and an up-to-date ministry plan. When concrete ministry projects and members' support in budgeting monies and other commitments come together, the congregation's dream will be advanced. A fair, open, and future-oriented budgeting process develops member morale and makes ministry more intentional.

Review Questions

1. How is budgeting related to dreaming and planning?
2. Which basic principles undergird budgeting?
3. What are the steps involved in a ministry action budgeting process?

Notes

1. Lyle E. Schaller, *Parish Planning* (Nashville: Abingdon Press, 1971), p. 38.
2. Waldo Beach, *The Christian Life* (Richmond: CLC Press, 1966), pp. 66-77.
3. These perspectives on ministry action budgeting are largely adapted from philosophies and materials developed by the Stewardship Commission, Suite 650, 901 Commerce Street, Nashville, TN 37203-3620.

A Selected Bibliography on Budgeting for Ministry Action

Chalk, Logan M. *Zero-Base Budgeting Comes of Age.* New York: AMACOM, 1977.

Cunningham, Richard B. *Creative Stewardship.* Nashville: Abingdon Press, 1979.

Myers, Marvin. *Managing the Business Affairs of the Church.* Nashville: Convention Press, 1981.

Powell, Robert R. *Managing Church Business Through Group Procedures.* Englewood Cliffs, N.J.: Prentice-Hall, Inc., 1964.

Sweeny, Allen, and Wesner, John N., Jr. *Budgeting Fundamentals for Nonfinancial Executives.* New York: AMACOM, 1975.

— 10 —

MANAGING DECISION-MAKING MEETINGS

SOME BUSINESS LEADERS complain about spending one thousand hours in meetings each year! Congregations don't have that many committee meetings or decision-making sessions, thank goodness. But since congregational meetings involve volunteers who typically pick and choose their meetings, planners of church meetings must carefully consider the sessions they must lead. These leaders know effective and productive meetings are roughly equal parts of content (what we will do) and climate (how we will do our ministries together). Note how the content and climate themes are interwoven in meetings, especially decision-making sessions.

Meetings Come in Different Shapes and Sizes

Congregations rarely lack for meetings. In some denominations, wherever there are two members, there seem to be three meetings! Not all meetings are alike; they have different purposes and varied structures. Effective leaders quickly learn how to size up and design meetings. Look at these types of meetings and what they require.

- *"How can we . . . ?" or decision-making meetings.*
Goal: Finding solutions based on available information.

Leader's Role: Orchestrate, inform, probe, and let the group do the exploration.

Leader's Actions: Listen. Mediate. Question. Keep the focus on the issue(s) at hand. Define the problem(s). Track down the cause of the problem. Expand the range of potential solutions. Encourage discussion. Evaluate options. Summarize conclusions. Delegate the responsibilities for implementation. Praise group members for their efforts and creativity.

- *"If we could do anything . . . !" or creative meetings.*

Goal: Generate as many ideas and options as possible.

Leader's Role: Draw on the creative juices of the entire group.

Leader's Actions: Define the issue, and then lead from a low profile. Elicit responses actively and nonverbally. Brainstorm. Think out loud. Record ideas quickly and accurately. Limit evaluation until all ideas are on the table. Appraise. Assign implementation tasks as needed. Thank participants for joining in and risking their ideas.

- *"Here's how to . . . ." or training meetings.*

Goal: Teach people, introduce new ideas, and demonstrate techniques.

Leader's Role: Structure the learning laboratory, input information, and develop participative educational activities.

Leader's Actions: Provide information and hands-on experiences. Use a variety of input and processing approaches. Solicit and use feedback. Critique results and methods. Praise and encourage your learners.

Some of the approaches that fit decision-making meetings also work well for creative, training, and other types of meetings. In this chapter, however, we'll concentrate on the decision-making meeting.

How to Chair a Decision-Making Meeting

Leaders frequently find themselves in the formal responsibility of chairing a decision-making meeting.

Here are some suggestions to consider before you call the meeting to order.[1]

• Determine the objective of the meeting. Know which decision must be made.
• Create a climate in which members never feel a need to defend themselves or their ideas.
• Listen carefully and judiciously. Helpful ideas and responses need to be spotlighted and built upon; negative, damaging, and valueless reactions need to be allowed to die quietly. Paraphrase member contributions accurately.
• Use your position power sparingly. A heavy hand often squelches promising alternatives and new ideas.
• Understand *Robert's Rules of Order* (or the parliamentary guide your congregation specifies) and use it fairly.
• Don't compete with group members. Most leaders find it difficult to offer their own ideas throughout a meeting without favoring their personal viewpoints.
• Keep your finger on the group's psychological pulse. One way to monitor your group's atmosphere is to pay attention to and probe laughter. Some humor elicits "minus laughter," which covers putdowns and masks hostility. Other humorous remarks demonstrate "plus laughter," a spontaneous appreciation of creative ideas.
• Involve every group member and all the gifts of the members. Ask for the contributions of quiet members. Deal firmly with dominators. (1) Break in and say, "Thanks for your ideas about . . . we have that contribution in our minds now." (2) When you ask for a response, don't make eye contact with compulsive talkers. (3) If the dominator persists, have a frank talk with the person and play a tape recording of the meeting, if you have made one.
• Plan your meetings carefully. Develop an agenda and use a meeting management model (see below).

When Are Meetings Necessary?

A meeting isn't the answer to every problem. However, several types of situations and goals lend themselves to the resources of meetings. Consider these possibilities for needed meetings. Call a meeting to . . .

● **Build community.** Community-building meetings are intended to generate team spirit and to keep the group's interest focused.

● **Solve problems.** Solution-seeking sessions create a setting where bits and pieces of information and experiences can be traded so that problems can be broadly analyzed and explanations discovered.

● **Make reports.** Reporting sessions indicate group progress. These meetings also show how problems common to the group are being approached. They stimulate discussion and action.

● **Unfold plans and projects.** These meetings provide information regarding the grand sweep of the congregation's dream and specify the next steps in implementing the vision.

● **Train members.** Training sessions attempt to increase the competence and confidence of workers, and, therefore, to enhance their value to the congregation at large.

● **Encourage action.** These meetings communicate and direct ministries members will engage in, when these actions will be attempted, and how this work is to be done.

● **Develop consensus.** Decision-making sessions open the choosing process to the information, opinions, and participation of members.

RSVP

Who should be invited to decision-making meetings? While participants vary somewhat from meeting to meeting, consider putting these persons on your list of invitees when decisions are at stake.

● Members who have information or skills appropriate to the issue at hand.

● Members who need information on the issue at hand.

● Leaders who have the official responsibility for implementing decisions.

• Members who must implement the group's decisions.
• Members who can make strategic linkages in the congregation and legitimize the decision to the broader membership.
• Members who have a positive attitude toward the issue to be decided.

A Model for Managing Decision-Making Meetings

Decision-making meetings call for broad participation, pooled resources, and crucial information supplied by experts, resource persons, and congregational leaders and legitimizers. Leaders need, therefore, to be evenhanded in style and balanced in content and viewpoint sharing. They help guide the group in defining and analyzing the core problem, researching the issue and building a factual base, generating and exploring options, putting the facts into context, summarizing conclusions, selecting an alternative, and implementing decisions.

A four-sequence model for managing decision-making meetings helps us provide catalytic leadership in groups. Evaluating, creating, deciding, and ministering pinpoint the four vital actions decision-making groups take. The "ministry cycle" process can be simply depicted.[2]

Each stage of the model works best with a Catalyst in the leader's chair. Catalysts participate actively in all the model's steps. Catalysts evaluate their group's history and progress. They share their ideas freely during the creative process. Catalysts also help the group decide on and implement their choices.

Catalysts influence most when they identify which stage on the model the group is in, sum up the group's movement, trigger the group's progress on to the next step in the process, and focus the group's energy on the appropriate level in the model's process. Catalysts use all the gifts and potential contributions of all group members.

A ministry cycle provides a framework for guiding decision-making meetings. This model lends two impor-

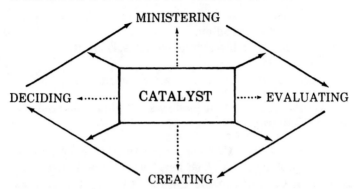

Illustration 21. Ministry Cycle for Meeting Management

tant resources for leaders: a mental picture of a meeting management process and a way to guide a process instead of attempting to control people. Let's examine each of the four stages individually.

(1) *Evaluating is the process of measuring performance against purpose.* When a meeting process begins with evaluation, the group clarifies where it stands in its progress and how well it has done its work to date. A range of evaluation options is available to meeting leaders.

- Specify the dream or part of the dream assigned to the group by the larger congregation.
- Pinpoint the group's task and mandate for action.
- Narrate the group's history and work to date.
- Identify the group's progress to this point in time.

(2) *Creating is the process of filtering options by generating and appraising alternatives.* Most meetings require some problem-solving to be done. Some system for attacking problems is helpful for group leaders. The IDEAL method provides one format. IDEAL is an easy-to-remember acrostic which structures a problem-solving approach.

1 3 1

I — Identify the problem.

D—Define that problem.

E—Explore possible strategies for solving it.

A—Act on your decision.

L—Look at the results of your solution.[3]

Several guidelines help leaders set the stage for creative problem solving.

• Generate at least three or four alternatives for solving specific problems. A frequent error problem-solving groups make is in considering too few potential options and closing on a solution too quickly. Poor solutions are developed in this manner. No other possible "Plan B's" are waiting in the wings to be applied if your preferred solution doesn't work out after all.

• Create a playful mood. Innovative solutions often spin off other more mundane possibilities. Creative decision makers structure time for ideas to be mulled over and even slept on. These leaders also encourage ideas to be manipulated, placed in other frameworks and settings, and related to seemingly unrelated concepts. Too tight a rein by the group leader inhibits generating creative options.

• Brainstorm potential solutions. Brainstorming requires a relaxed setting, the freedom of risking far out thoughts for public critique, a willingness to suspend judgment until all ideas have been posted, and the encouragement to let ideas spark even better ideas.

• Polish the best potential solutions by stretching and tailoring these ideas. Another acrostic, SCAMPER, helps to expand existing concepts and develop new ones.

(3) *Deciding is the process of selecting a solution to challenges facing the group.* Judgment must be passed on options if the congregation is to pursue its dream. Therefore, some clear-eyed realists and well informed leaders need to help the congregation choose its best alternative and prepare to act on that solution.

S—Substitute. What can you substitute for this idea?
C—Combine. What can you combine with this idea?
A—Adapt. What can be adapted from this idea?
M—Magnify, miniaturize, multiply. How can this idea be expanded, shrunk, or increased?
P—Put to other uses. How can this idea be given another application?
E—Else? What else? Where else? How else?
R—Rearrange or reverse? Can elements of this idea be rearranged or reversed?[4]

• The congregation's dream provides a baseline for decision-making. The vision of ministry represents a deep and basic value for the congregation.
• Who should be involved in making decisions? Here's the fundamental principle. Everyone who will be expected to help implement the decision deserves to be included in making the initial decision.
• Use settings that separate decision-making from consensus building. Because decision-making creates pressure, some leaders like to plan some idea and information sharing sessions apart from the need to decide immediately. This kind of forum elicits helpful input, gathers feedback about the mood and implementation limits of the congregation, and builds momentum for taking constructive action on the decision.
• Make group decisions by consensus, when possible. Voting gets the group's reaction fast. However, voting divides the group and sometimes dooms later implementation chances. Deciding by consensus requires more patience from the leader and more time from both leaders and followers.

(4) *Ministering is the process of implementing the congregation's decisions, plans, and dreams.* The Bible reminds us that "faith by itself, if it has no works, is dead" (Jas. 2:17). When decisions have been made by the congregation, the call to ministry action is natural and needed.

Agenda: Necessary Structure for Effective Meetings

A meeting has an agenda—whether it is explicit or only implied. Effective meetings often use the structure an agenda provides. What should be considered in developing an agenda for a meeting?

- List the overall objective of the meeting.
- Itemize the specific issues to be dealt with at the meeting.
- Sequence agenda items carefully by scheduling the toughest challenges early in the meeting.
- Present the agenda visually.
- Put time limits on the agenda so the meeting has both a starting and an ending time.

Reminders for Meeting Management

Good meetings don't just happen. They are thought about, planned for, and carefully led. Use the reminders below as a checklist for planning and managing meetings.

- Start and adjourn on time.
- Prepare fully in order to exude confidence and show appropriate enthusiasm.
- Pace the meeting. Keep things moving ahead smoothly and deliberately.
- Apply the Golden Rule. Diplomacy pays.
- Use humor naturally to change the mood and rate of progress of sessions.
- Pay attention to both the task at hand and the morale of the group members.
- Develop a comfortable meeting management model.

Overview: Managing Decision-Making Meetings

Content and climate are both key themes in ministry meetings. Decision-making sessions deserve careful planning, a competent chairperson, an appropriate occasion or need, an agenda, and broadly selected participants. Effective leaders of meetings apply a meeting management model to the issues their group is exploring. Then their groups can proceed confidently and productively.

Review Questions

1. What kinds of common congregational meetings are ministers called on to lead?
2. When are meetings necessary?
3. What are the four basic leader actions in guiding decision-making meetings?

Notes

1. George M. Prince, "How to Be a Better Meeting Chairman," *Harvard Business Review* (January-February 1969), pp. 98-108.
2. Robert D. Dale, *Ministers as Leaders* (Nashville: Broadman Press, 1984), pp. 113-17. All rights reserved. Used by permission.
3. John Bransford and Barry S. Stein, *The IDEAL Problem Solver* (New York: W. H. Freeman, n.d.).
4. Charles H. Clark, *Idea Management: How to Motivate Creativity and Innovation* (New York: AMACOM, 1980), p. 16.

A Selected Bibliography for Managing Decision-Making Meetings

Anderson, Philip A. *Church Meetings That Matter.* Philadelphia: United Church Press, 1965.

Carnes, William T. *Effective Meetings for Busy People: Let's Decide It and Go Home.* New York: McGraw-Hill, 1980.

Johnson, Luke T. *Decision Making in the Church: A Biblical Approach.* Philadelphia: Fortress Press, 1983.

Jones, O. Garfield. *Parliamentary Procedure at a Glance.* New York: Hawthorn Books, 1971.

O'Connell, Brian. *Effective Leadership in Voluntary Organizations.* Chicago: Follett Publishing Co., 1976.

— 11 —

BUILDING
MINISTRY TEAMS

UNIFYING DIVERSE PERSONS and tasks is team-building. Support, respect, interdependency, and *esprit de corps* are crucial ingredients of teamwork and are needed whenever two or more church members must depend on one another.

Leadership is vital to all ministry efforts. In team-building, however, leadership becomes a shared responsibility. Consider this example from the world of nature. When geese migrate south toward the rice fields of the American Gulf Coast, they always fly in a "V" formation. Two engineers used a wind tunnel to calculate why the "V" formation is continually used by the birds. Each goose, by flapping its wings, creates lift for the bird that follows. Overall, the flock gains 71 percent greater flying range as a team than when flying alone. One goose "takes the point" and flies at the front of the formation for a while and then falls back into a less taxing position in the flock. During a long journey, each goose flies the point at some time. In all kinds of situations, teamwork calls for shared, timely leadership.

Team-building has clear theological roots.[1] For example, Paul's image of the church as Christ's body reminds us of several vital truths about team-building.

● Congregations are varied and diverse. They require coordination and leadership (Rom. 12:4, 6).

● Diversity enriches. All the varied parts of the body are needed in order for the organism to function properly (1 Cor. 12:14-26).

● Christ himself unifies the church (1 Cor. 12:12-13). The person and example of Christ provide coherence for ministry teams.

Jesus used ministry teams. He sent out his disciples two by two (Mark 6:7). He called the twelve apostles for training and ministry action. Today we continue to use the the team pattern for ministry too. We enlist teams for outreach and evangelism, to co-chair work groups, to form clergy teams on church staffs, and to represent congregations as delegates or messengers at regional and national gatherings of denominations.

When Is Team-building Needed?

Team-building is needed in congregations when two or more persons are required to relate to one another and to work together. In other words, team-building is necessary for both enriching Christian community and doing ministry. What are some signals that team-building is timely?

Team-building is needed when . . .

. . . committees and members are getting in each other's way and duplicating efforts.

. . . leaders are doing all the work and teetering on the brink of burnout.

. . . members' pet projects are getting attention, but the overall goals of the congregation receive little spotlight.

. . . there's little enthusiasm for the ministries of the church.

. . . work keeps falling through the cracks, and ministry is left undone.

. . . meetings are boring and unproductive.

. . . leaders spend too much time checking up on why things haven't been done.

. . . no one knows what's going on.

Sound familiar? If so, your congregation is a prime candidate for team-building.

When Are Teams Effective?

Teams or committees aren't needed for all ministry situations; individuals can work alone with better results in some cases. But teams and groups are superior to individuals in many circumstances.[2] Here are four varied situations when teams are helpful.

• Sequential solutions—Some tasks call for sequential, or one-step-at-a-time, solutions. Teams are less apt to overlook necessary steps than one person. It's the old idea that "two heads are better than one."
• Vague situations—When problems are ambiguous or when potential solutions can't be proven in advance, groups are better able to explore, clarify, and test options.
• Social reasons—Teams place us with others whose company we enjoy or whose ideas stimulte us. Individuals need others for affirmation and relational contact.
• Safety factors—Risks are inherent in decision-making. Groups lessen the possibilities of failure and protect us from the full responsibility for mistakes.

Skills and Models for Team-building

Teams rarely develop automatically. Whether a church committee, a family, an athletic squad, a symphony orchestra, a spaceship launch, or a ballet troupe is under consideration, teamwork is basic and calls for leadership. Skilled leaders aid team-building processes by (1) keeping the dream of the congregation before the smaller work groups within the church (see chapters 6 and 7), (2) maintaining a corporate overview of the congregation's goals, needs, and opportunities, and (3) setting a congregational climate of cooperation, collaboration, and coordination. Management and leadership skills merge especially in team development.

Two broad families of team-building approaches are available to congregational leaders. A relational model places interpersonal concerns in the foreground and production issues in the background.[3] This model uses a four-step cycle to build teams and is preferred by many Encourager-styled and some Catalyst leaders.

- Sharing basic relationship information.
- Affirming personal abilities and contributions to group work.
- Setting work goals.
- Celebrating progress and goal attainment.

Relational team-building models require basic group enrichment skills. (1) Relational team-builders facilitate rather than direct. They acknowledge each team member's contribution to team efforts. They remind the group of a range of options to the challenges they face. They suggest potential links between the ideas of group members. (2) Relational team-builders keep the group from jumping to solutions too quickly and overlooking constructive alternatives. (3) Relational team-builders protect minority opinion and keep opposing points of view from being excluded or devaluated. In this approach, leaders are like gentle cops who guide discussion by keeping one topic at a time before the group and by nudging the group along in orderly fashion and on schedule.

Fellowship enrichment and deepening friendships are two outcomes of this style of team-building. On a one-to-one scale, Jesus' encounters with Nicodemus (John 3) and Zacchaeus (Luke 19) as well as Barnabas' intercession for Paul (Acts 9) trace the broader contours of the relational style of team development.

A task-oriented model of team-building, on the other hand, focuses on production. In this approach, the job becomes the guide for the team-building process; individual goals and other concerns are subordinated to getting the job done.[4] Many Commanders and some Catalyst leaders are comfortable with this style of team-building.

Task-oriented team-building involves several steps:

- Determining the congregation's fundamental goal.
- Creating an organizational climate that makes people feel it's safe to speak up without fear of attack or accusation.
- Securing the agreement of team members to cooperate rather than compete.
- Getting commitments from all members to work toward and contribute to reaching the congregation's vision of itself.
- Allowing the dream of the church to dictate which tactics, projects, and programs will be used to reach the goals of the congregation.
- Forging workable compromises when disagreements arise.
- Implementing plans and acting as cheerleader for group successes.

Task-oriented team-building is demonstrated in the work of Thomas Edison. Early in his creative career Edison decided to pour his energies only into inventions that were commercially marketable. Working from that stance, Edison created his famous Menlo Park Laboratory and recruited a technical team. This approach served as a prototype for the giant industrial laboratories General Electric and Bell later developed. The significance of Edison's lab and his creative team is simple: the job became the boss, and the leader worked with the entire team to complete the task.

Congregations are collections of teams, staff groups, and committees. Each task group depends to some degree on other congregational leaders and work groups. Let's take one work group—the church staff—and remind ourselves of how church staff ministers fit into the congregational team.

Memo to Laypersons:
Staff Ministers Are Team Leaders

Every church has its staff. Not all are ordained, employed clergy. In fact, the majority of church staffs are mostly made up of volunteers. How church leaders—especially the church staff—treat one another and work as a team sets the pace for the larger membership of the church. That's an important climate setter for your congregation. What constructive understandings can guide laypersons' thinking about church staff relationships?

• *Church staff leaders are people, not slots on an organizational chart.* Some people set clergy apart from the rest of the world. As one misinformed church member described his view of the world, "There are three kinds of people in the world—men, women, and clergy." God's children, not excluding clergypersons, are ordinary creaturs responding to an unique calling. Church staffers need support, growth opportunities, and a clear sense of congregational goals in order to be effective team leaders.
• *The quality of church staff relationships varies widely.* Some staffs relate comfortably and work well. Others nettle each other and aren't very productive. Why? In part, it's because some leaders, like most Encouragers and some Catalysts, are primarily concerned with "identity bonds" and are, consequently, more attuned to relational matters. Others like most Commanders and some Catalysts, conversely, feed off "task bonds" and stay centered on production goals for the most part. When staff leaders recognize that some persons are identity related and others task related, an effective and deliberate team mesh can be negotiated and balanced out. In all cases, understanding undergirds the quality of staff relationships.

141

• *Specialist and generalist leaders can work well together—if they know their gifts and fill their roles.* To paraphrase the motto of Harry Truman, the buck has to stop somewhere. Someone, usually the pastor, must see "the big picture" and maintain an overall corporate perspective on the congregation's life and work. This generalist stance provides a framework for staff ministers with distinctive and narrower skills to use their specialties to build up the body of Christ (Eph. 4:12).

• *The more staff members you have, the higher the odds are of interpersonal tension.* Large staffs don't automatically disagree. However, relational links multiply geometrically and become noticeably more complicated as staff ranks grow. A mathematical formula can be applied to this phenomenon.

> The number of staffers
> times that number minus one
> divided by two
> equals the total potential relational bonds.

For instance, using this formula, we find that
a staff of two persons contains only one primary bond
($2 \times 1 \div 2 = 1$),
a staff of four contains six bonds ($4 \times 3 \div 2 = 6$),
a staff of ten contains forty-five bonds, and
a staff of twenty contains one hundred ninety bonds.

The old saying, "The more, the merrier," applies to total staff resources more easily than to relationships. As more staffers are added, relationships become potentially more complicated. Staff selection, team-building, and enriching staff relationships become, of necessity, a higher congregational priority.

• *Clear job descriptions for each staff position formalize congregational expectations for both employed and volun-*

teer leaders. Job descriptions provide the skeletons for the flesh and blood of teamwork.

● *Healthy staff relationshps provide a balance of freedom and security*. Teams need both space to freelance and limits to keep us focused.

● *Staffs deserve development*. No one is perfect. We all need growth in some area or areas of ministry. Most of us can overcome our limits if a developmental approach is taken toward us. Congregations can encourage development and make resources available for continuing education and skill enhancement. Additionally, forums for communication, feedback, evaluation, and planning keep the staff and congregation in touch with the needs and concerns of each other.

Some church staffs include an especially challenging role—the assistant or associate minister. How can the subordinate role be viewed on a church staff team?

Assistant: How Difficult Is This Role?

Many folks who fill an assistant's role feel some dissatisfaction with secondary positions. Bridesmaids dream of becoming brides. Runners-up want to win the next contest. Second bananas want to become the stars of the show. One vice-president of the United States described his job as being "as worthless as a bucket of warm spit." Just how difficult is the assistant role?

Secondary roles on teams are a mixed bag of advantages and disadvantages:

● You have some responsibility. But, you have neither ultimate responsibility nor exposure to failure; you're sheltered to some degree.

● You gain experience. But you avoid taking the risks of leadership by yourself; your supervisor provides a human buffer of security.

● You can exercise initiative. On the other hand, your authority is limited. You will feel the frustration of being requested (or demanded) to do things you don't have the power to produce.

• You are under supervision. That's a protected position and a supportive relationship. The catch? To be happy and productive, you need a good supervisor. Unfortunately, not all church staff supervisors work well with their teams.

Relating to a Difficult Supervisor

Church staffs and ministry teams experience the same internal stresses and strains as other work groups. On occasion, those difficulties center around supervision approaches. How can church staff ministers relate more comfortably with supervisors who are suspicious, wishy-washy, too bossy, or too controlling? Here are some coping strategies.

• *Understand your supervisor's ministry style.* You don't have to like your supervisor's approach to working relationships, but you're more apt to relate to your supervisor better if you are clear about how your supervisor thinks and works.

Consider basic leader style preferences. Does your supervisor appreciate teamwork and cooperation (like a Catalyst)? Does your supervisor give orders and tell you directly or indirectly that he or she is boss (like a Commander)? Does your supervisor show concern and support for you (like an Encourager)? Does your supervisor withdraw from staff relationships behind a closed office door and play emotional "hide-and-seek" in meetings (like the Hermit)? Becoming clear about how your supervisor tries to lead gives you a beginning point for improving your working relationships.

Look at your supervisor's work patterns too. Which of these possibilities fits your supervisor? Likes to begin work early? Prefers to stay late? Wants lots of meetings? Hates meetings? Likes short, structured meetings? Enjoys leisurely, flexible meetings? Wants titles and formality to be evident? Prefers first names and informality? Is a stickler for deadlines? Adapts completion times to unexpected occurrences? Wants details in reports and final products? Is at ease with broad concepts and the contours of ideas and projects? Focuses on production and results? Prefers people and relationships? You see the picture. Watch until you understand how your supervisor thinks and works. You'll gain an important overview from answering these and similar questions. As Yogi Berra observed, "You can tell an awful lot just by watching."

You don't have to agree fully with your supervisor's approaches to staff work, but you'll be more comfortable if you can understand and anticipate your supervisor's patterns.

• *Know who you are and how you work best.* Ask yourself the same kinds of questions that are listed above. Effective staff relationships involve a comfortable meshing of personalities and work styles. You'll contribute more to good supervisor-supervisee relationships when you know what special attributes or particular irritants you bring to the staff mix yourself.

• *Discover the congregation's overall vision and your supervisor's goals.* The congregation's vision of ministry provides the lodestar for church staff functioning. The dream of the church points the direction for staff ministry—both clergy and lay. Observe, moreover, how your supervisor intends to contribute to the congregation's dream. Talk about that common vision with your supervisor. Then you'll be more apt to stay in step with the congregation and your supervisor's expectations.

• *Don't surprise your supervisor.* Work flow depends on accurate, up-to-date information. Keep your supervisor posted on the progress of projects. Since most of us don't like to hear bad news anyway, we may hesitate to tell supervisors when we've made a mistake or when there's a disaster in the making. Negative information is even more vital to supervisors, however, because immediate adjustments may be needed to keep bad situations from becoming worse.

• *Recognize that you are a subordinate in this relationship.* Our work relationships vary. Some are friendly, peer relationships. Others place you in charge. In those cases when you are under supervision, accept the fact that someone has been assigned the organizational responsibility of overseeing your work. The structure has been set. Guard against counter-dependent behaviors that smack of rebellion and conflict. Focus on improving your relationship with your supervisor rather than centering your frustrations on the congregation's organizational structure or personnel policies. Healthy relationships have a way of leavening "the system" for the better.

• *Demonstrate personal and professional integrity.* Apply the Golden Rule. Relate to your fellow church staffers fairly. Deal with everyone honestly. Don't promise what you can't deliver. If you miss a deadline, inform those persons whose work depends on you and your work. In other words, be a dependable team player and teamwork will go better.

Overview: Team-building

Team-building turns diversity into unity. While teamwork isn't necessary for all situations, some ministry circumstances call for teams. Both relational and task-oriented approaches are available and useful to ministry leaders. Church staffs are special types of ministry teams and call for care, cultivation, and quality supervision.

Review Questions

1. When is team-building needed in a congregation?
2. What situations call for the efforts of ministry teams rather than individual members?
3. Can you describe two models of team-building?
4. What kind of leadership issues do church staff teams face?

Notes

1. Robert D. Dale, *Ministers as Leaders* (Nashville: Broadman Press, 1984), pp. 99-100.
2. Ron Zemke, "Committees: Will Forming One Really Help?" *Training*, February 1978, p. 24.
3. Dale, *Ministers as Leaders*, pp. 104-6.
4. Irwin M. Rubin, Mark S. Plovnick, and Ronald E. Fry, *Task-Oriented Team Development* (New York: McGraw-Hill, 1981).

Selected Bibliography on Team-building

Dale, Robert D. *Ministers as Leaders.* Nashville: Broadman Press, 1984.
Dyer, William G. *Team Building: Issues and Alternatives.* Reading, Mass.: Addison-Wesley Publishing Co., 1977.
Fordyce, Jack, and Weil, Raymond. *Managing with People.* Reading, Mass.: Addison-Wesley Publishing Co., 1971.
Rubin, Irwin M.; Plovnick, Mark S.; and Fry, Ronald E. *Task-Oriented Team Development.* New York: McGraw-Hill, 1981.
Zemke, Ron. "Team Building: Helping People Learn to Work Together," *Training,* February 1978, pp. 23-34.

— 12 —

MOTIVATING MINISTRY VOLUNTEERS

SECULAR STUDIES OF how workers accept responsibility help church leaders think about motivation in congregational settings. For example, a 1973 study of 19,000 respondents conducted at Case Western University yielded an interesting ranking of motivational factors.

#1—Interesting work
#2—Good pay
#3—Seeing the results of their work
#4—Chance to use their minds
#5—Chance to develop skills/abilities
#6—Participation in work-related decisions
#7—Recognition for a job well done

The ranking continues on through fifteen items. But these top seven concerns suggest some handles on motivational challenges in volunteer settings. To illustrate, match these motivational actions with each of the key motivators mentioned above.

#1—The range of possible ministry assignments in and beyond congregations is virtually endless. Effective leaders are alert to opportunities to match members' interests and gifts with absorbing ministry needs. The good match of abilities and needs makes for "interesting work."

#2—Volunteers aren't paid in money or benefits. They do, however, receive spiritual and psychological payoffs. "Good pay" makes for active and fulfilled volunteers.

#3—Doing an entire task from beginning to end is generally a motivator. For example, Volvo discovered their workers preferred not to work on the old-fashioned assembly lines with their repetitive tasks. Rather, these Volvo workers built a better quality car and were more highly satisfied when small teams built one complete automobile from start to finish.

#4—Solving problems and relating to fellow workers is always a challenging experience. Some coaching and training may be needed, but there's no shortage of opportunities to use our minds in ministry to others.

#5—Pre-service as well as on-the-job training programs help persons in ministry to work confidently and effectively. Growth is motivational to most Christians.

#6—Participative decision-making is usually motivational. When groups select their own goals, the individual members of the decision-making team are apt to join in implementing their decisions.

#7—Saying "thank you" is a motivational act. Surprisingly, this basic act of appreciation and recognition is too often overlooked in congregations. While we will be rewarded with a "well done" in heaven, a little earthly thanks is also rewarding.

What Motivates People?

The most motivated persons, not the most talented, have made history, claims management theorist Peter Drucker. He may be right. It is clear that human beings are always motivated to do something. What kind of things motivate people?

Theories of motivation fall into two broad categories: external and internal. *External,* sometimes called extrinsic, approaches claim that we do what we do to gain rewards or to avoid punishment. The "carrot-on-the-end-of-a-stick" pursuit of rewards or the "God's going to get you for that" threat of punishment are illustrations of external motives. *Internal,* otherwise referred to as intrinsic, theories describe motivation as coming from within the individual. The internal theories say that people do what they do because ultimately they want and choose to.

By and large, Christian leaders don't rely on external motivation methods. Volunteers simply cease to volunteer when they feel enticed by artificial rewards or threatened by manipulative punishments. In most churches, manipulation doesn't work in practice and is also questionable on theological grounds. Pushing followers constantly soon discourages them or wears them out. The "swift kick in the seat of the pants" school of motivation is usually as ineffective over the long haul in churches as the "froth and frenzy" approach. The latter style is, however, popular with enthusiastic and energetic leaders who feel public hyperactivity excites followers. A friend of mine favors the "froth and frenzy" method; he claims he's so active in the pulpit that he has to wear his jogging shoes when he preaches!

The differences between volunteers and employees suggest several major reasons external approaches to motivation don't work well in congregations. For starters, *payment* is different. Volunteers—to the surprise of many persons—are "paid" in recognition, personal development, and service; employees gain wages and fringe benefits. The *outcomes* volunteers and employees hope for are different too. Volunteers want to help others or grow themselves; employees simply do a job. The sense of *enjoyment* may also be different for these two categories of workers. Volunteers usually like what they do and want to serve—otherwise they wouldn't volunteer. Employees may neither like what they do nor, except for economic necessity, really want to do it. When church leaders take an employer-employee stance toward volunteers, they can drive their fellow workers away with external motivation methods. These leaders misunderstand their followers and overuse external motivation's "pull" methods.

Internal motivation approaches generally fit congregational settings and volunteers' needs better. Here's how two types of intrinsic motivation theories work. The *deficiency* model of motivation emphasizes the internal "push" of needs, wants, tensions, and discomforts. Obviously, hungry persons are motivated to seek food. (Occasionally, some leaders decide to keep others hungry in order to manipulate these unfortunates. This tactic is unethical and unthinkable for church leaders.) Other persons are motivated by their internal needs to achieve; they want to get things done successfully. Some want to influence followers and exercise power. Still others seek warm, positive relationships with others; they need a sense of belonging and, consequently, reach out for group membership.

Another type of internal motivation involves *growth* models. The best-known growth theory of motivation is Abraham Maslow's hierarchy of needs.[1]

This approach to motivation notes that human beings have at least five major categories of needs: physical, safety, social, ego, and self-actualization. The hierarchy of needs claims the most basic unmet need is the motivator. When a need is satisfied, that need ceases to motivate and another motive level is triggered. The movement through the range of motives is generally upward unless some lower level need occurs again.

Two suggestions about the hierarchy of needs understanding of motivation may help leaders. (1) Leaders must be very sensitive to the real needs of their followers, or they will miss the operational motives of others. Leaders are often more highly (and differently) motivated than followers. This potential difference calls for special insight into others' needs by leaders. (2) Sometimes the broader needs of the society shift rather quickly. If the congregation reflects the larger picture of the culture, the motivational needs of the membership will likely change too. Leaders may "go to sleep at the switch" during times of societal upheaval and miss the emerging needs of their

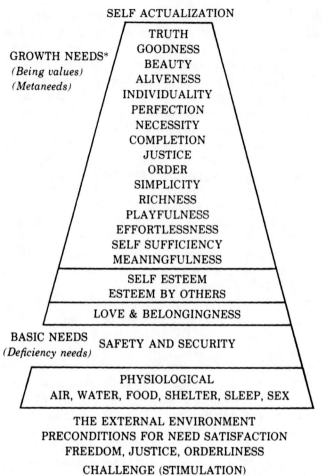

SELF ACTUALIZATION

GROWTH NEEDS*
(Being values)
(Metaneeds)

TRUTH
GOODNESS
BEAUTY
ALIVENESS
INDIVIDUALITY
PERFECTION
NECESSITY
COMPLETION
JUSTICE
ORDER
SIMPLICITY
RICHNESS
PLAYFULNESS
EFFORTLESSNESS
SELF SUFFICIENCY
MEANINGFULNESS

SELF ESTEEM
ESTEEM BY OTHERS

LOVE & BELONGINGNESS

BASIC NEEDS
(Deficiency needs) SAFETY AND SECURITY

PHYSIOLOGICAL
AIR, WATER, FOOD, SHELTER, SLEEP, SEX

THE EXTERNAL ENVIRONMENT
PRECONDITIONS FOR NEED SATISFACTION
FREEDOM, JUSTICE, ORDERLINESS
CHALLENGE (STIMULATION)
*Growth needs are all of equal importance (not hierarchical)

Illustration 22. Maslow's Hierarchy of Needs

followers. For example, during the 1973 oil embargo we discovered to our surprise that fully one-third of our congregation's members were experiencing day-to-day difficulty paying their bills. We quickly offered some budgeting and family financial planning sessions in our

Christian education program. These rapidly designed sessions were extremely well attended. (I don't remember what the sermon topics had been before that time frame, but I'm reasonably sure that money management hadn't been the primary theme. It's easy for leaders to assume their needs are others' needs too and miss motivational opportunities.) Needs and, therefore, motives can change rapidly.

Assumptions Behind Effective Motivation

Theory grows out of assumptions. Assumptions are the positions we take without examining them. Since we don't check our assumptions, they can betray us. Wise leaders, therefore, check their assumptions in order to work from healthy and wholesome stances toward their followers.

• Motivation is internal and inherent. We are dynamic, ever-wanting beings. Motivation is, therefore, a matter of direction, not movement.
• Unsatisfied needs are motivators. Leaders help followers discover and meet their legitimate needs.
• Matching members' needs and organizational goals isn't automatic. Leaders live between two temptations. They are tempted to use people for the sake of the organization or to allow the organization to drift while people's individual needs become paramount.
• The Holy Spirit is the Christian's primary motivator. The Spirit of Christ indwells and energizes us. The Spirit provides an internal support system and empowers us. Therefore, the Holy Spirit becomes our primary "need-meeting" resource.

Building a Congregational Climate for Motivation

The primary motivational actions of leaders (who follow the internal theories) revolve around creating an organizational climate in which motivated members can invest

1 5 3

their energies. Several climate building steps are available to church leaders. The ideas below are listed randomly and are offered as an array of resources.

• Keep the congregation's dream of ministry clearly defined and publicly expressed. The goals and values of the group should be selected by group members so they can act in service to their dream. Leaders who keep the dream keenly focused, advocated, and expressed in words, actions, and symbols create a motivational climate. (For more information on sharpening congregational vision, see chapter 7).

• Create an atmosphere of affirmation. Some leaders refer to this atmosphere as a "high stroke" climate. That is, members feel recognized and appreciated. These volunteers are well paid in "thank you's" and positive reinforcement. Volunteers can't be thanked enough for quality work.

There's an interesting flip side to this principle. When leaders feel overworked and underappreciated, they become stroke deprived and relate irrationally and uncharacteristically. They may suspect their followers have become "yes men" who withhold their candor and tailor their feedback to what they think are the interests of the leader. Leaders get a little (or a lot) crazy under these circumstances. Wise followers will make sure that the atmosphere of affirmation includes the leader team for their own safety and for the well-being of their organization. Unaffirmed leaders are inconsistent leaders.

• Identify the energy reservoirs of your congregation. Key clues to motivation in an organization are the pockets of enthusiasm it contains. For example, you may find an especially active and effective evangelism committee or an almost fanatical adult choir or an active youth group in your church. They are reservoirs of energy and motivation. Since motivation is a crucial commodity in congregations, it needs to be identified and channeled toward mainstream ministries that contribute to the basic dream of the church.

- Work to align members' individual needs with the goals of the congregation. Church management stresses the achievement of formal organizational goals. Christian leadership also spotlights the importance of pursuing the informal needs of members as they spontaneously emerge. When personal "I want's" and organizational "we need's" are lined up, progress will be made because motivation is obviously present.

- Help your followers recognize and meet their legitimate needs. People enjoy being part of an organization they get something meaningful from. Take the common need we have for structure in our lives as an example. Structure and organization help us manage anxiety and change. To illustrate, an order of worship lends structure to corporate worship services. We need to know what comes now and what comes next. Then we can put aside our concerns about doing something at the wrong time, relax, and enter fully into the flow of the service.

- Build ministry teams. Church members enjoy feeling we have a genuine contribution to make to our group. We support ministry efforts we've helped plan and create. We accept delegated responsibilities when the tasks match our skills and interests. A sense of "we're in this together" is a key ingredient in a motivational climate. (For more information on building ministry teams, see chapter 11.)

- Eliminate demotivators.[2] Irritants distract us from productive service. These so-called "hygiene factors" may invade churches in the form of rowdy youth or poor ventilation or worship services that last past lunchtime. Such hygiene factors demotivate us and need to be offset or eliminated. Fortunately, most irritants are related to our worship and work environments and can, therefore, be more easily dealt with than bothersome or apathetic personalities in the congregation.[3]

- Encourage participative decision-making. We (and others) feel emotional ownership in projects we develop.

We are motivated to carry through with plans we take part in making in the first place.

• Contract for action. We like to know what's expected of us, be able to negotiate some points, and agree on our privileges and responsibilities. Contracts are the interpersonal agreements that shape and make reliable the behaviors of persons in ministry teams. These covenants or promises put handles on working relationships and help us clarify expectations.

Are You Motivated?

Are you motivated? Sure you are. You want something all the time. But are there some things you can do to focus your motivational energies more carefully? Consider some of these possibilities.

• Set specific goals.
• Spell out in writing your plans for pursuing your goals.
• Be realistic about your goals. Don't set goals so far beyond your reach that you have less than a fifty-fifty chance of attaining them.
• Choose a starting point and begin now! Do first things first.
• Tackle your toughest tasks at your peak times of the day.
• Set a deadline for each goal. Then establish intervening checkpoints too.
• Break your goal down into small projects so you won't be overwhelmed by enormous tasks.
• Don't confuse "I can't" and "I don't want to."
• List the overall benefits of reaching your goals. Reward yourself for successfully meeting your intermediate objectives.
• If you get stuck on some project, decide on one next step and move on. Don't let progress on all fronts grind to a halt.
• Remain optimistic. When you trip, laugh, then get up, and move on again.

Overview

Motivating volunteers calls for different theories, clear theological assumptions, and different motivational approaches. In congregational settings, internal theories and climate-building actions lend themselves to motivation. Self-motivation techniques are also useful in pursuing personal goals.

Review Questions

1. Can you distinguish between external and internal motivation theories?
2. What are your assumptions about human motivation?
3. Which motivational climate builders have you used most successfully?

Notes

1. Abraham H. Maslow, *Motivation and Personality* (New York: Harper & Row, 1970).
2. Fredrick Herzberg, *Work and the Nature of Man* (New York: World Publishing Co., 1966).
3. Robert D. Dale, *Surviving Difficult Church Members* (Nashville: Abingdon Press, 1984), pp. 86-101.

A Selected Bibliography on Motivating Volunteers

Herzberg, Fredrick. *Work and the Nature of Man.* New York: World Publishing Co., 1966.
Maslow, Abraham H. *Motivation and Personality.* New York: Harper & Row, 1970.
McDonough, Reginald M. *Keys to Effective Motivation.* Nashville: Broadman Press, 1979.
McGregor, Douglas. *The Human Side of Enterprise.* New York: McGraw-Hill, 1960.
Savage, John. *The Apathetic and Bored Church Member.* Pittsford, N.Y.: LEAD Consultants, 1976.

— *13* —

RESOLVING CONGREGATIONAL CONFLICTS

THERE'S AN OLD Sanskrit saying that wisely counsels knowing how you characteristically face anger and conflict:

> The anger of a good man
>   lasts an instant;
> that of a meddler
>   two hours;
> that of a base man
>   a day and a night;
> and that of a great sinner
>   until death.

When the anger of one or a few is multiplied congregation-wide, resolving conflict becomes a sticky challenge for church leaders.

Some circumstances require a direct, even angry, response. For example, Jesus was angered by sick religion (Matt. 23; Mark 3:1-6 and 11:15-16; John 2:13-22). He confronted those situations and persons who sponsored unhealthy religious practices. But even confronting sick religion and other perversions of faith calls for church leaders to become peacemakers ultimately. In congregations, collaboration, not competition or confrontation, is the healthiest long-term atmosphere for effective ministry.

When Christians Disagree

Congregational conflict surprises and disappoints many church members. Why? Because we view congregations idealistically. We want the body of Christ to be a perfect community. In the real world, however, congregations are made up of imperfect persons who live in an imperfect world. We Christians (and other humans) vividly demonstrate the doctrine of original sin in the workings of the institutions we establish.

Average persons spend an estimated 30 percent of our time dealing with some kind of conflict. Our roles vary across a spectrum from combatant to peacemaker. Whatever our stake in congregational conflicts, managing differences and diversity is a necessary skill for church leaders today.

What is conflict? Generally, conflict is pictured as something serious, intense, disruptive, and unpleasant. Do you think of conflict in any (or all) of the following terms? Collisions. Disagreements. Controversies. Quarrels. Battles. Struggles. Inevitable events. Sign of a vital organization. In many cases, all these descriptions apply to some extent. Literally, conflict means "to strike together." For our purposes, conflict occurs when (1) two or more competitors (2) decide their goals and/or values can be attained by one side but not by both (3) and take overt action to reach their goals and/or values to the exclusion of others' goals and/or values.

Types of Congregational Conflict

Broadly viewed, there are two types of congregational conflict: conflict over facts and conflicts involving feelings. Most disagreements blend both facts and feelings. But, in many cases, either facts or feelings predominate and require distinctive styles of resolution as noted below.

Facts——Negotiating
Feelings——Ventilating

Fact-based conflicts revolve around role conflict, philosophical differences, lack of cooperation, or competition for leadership. Factual differences call for cognitive resolution approaches, such as, negotiating, bargaining, and problem solving, to resolve their difficulties. Feeling-oriented differences center around incompatible personalities, blocked personal or interpersonal needs, and differences or similarities over leader style. Emotional conflicts use effective resolution techniques, such as, ventilating, mirroring, and exploring our states of mind.[1]

Dealing with Factual Controversies

Several basic steps provide a framework for resolving factual differences. A rough sequence is implied in the following guidelines.

• Develop a concrete problem statement. Pinpointing the fundamental disagreement between parties specifies a starting line for working through the conflict.
• Agree on a problem-solving process. If at least the next step in the reconciliation process can be selected by both sides, a process is unfolding. Planning mutual actions lends momentum to the conflict resolution process.
• Identify and build on common points of agreement. Even in intense conflict situations, some goals, issues, or values may be held by both sides and can be expanded. These positions provide a kind of integrative glue to both draw and hold antagonists together.
• Brainstorm a range of new solutions. The more possibilities mutual problem solvers can generate, the more options they have available when looking for solutions.

A Tool Kit for Factual Conflicts

An assortment of negotiation-oriented conflict management techniques can be used to deal with factual disagreements. The catalog of approaches below is listed in random order and is intended to provide a sample "tool kit" for peacemakers.

• Lay out a timeline. A full sequence of events helps in analyzing what has happened and where events went awry. Timelines help clarify what happened when to whom. The process of objectfying actions and reactions lends a basis for untangling and examining a disagreement.

• Make a bug list. Conflicts are full of circumstances that "bug" us. Listing these factors identifies the troublesome concerns. This approach gathers information on how each side in a disagreement views the other. Each side lists "how we see them" and "how we think they see us" on large sheets of newsprint. Post the sheets, ask everyone to scan the sheets, invite one member of each group to summarize their statements, and then discuss any misperceptions and stereotypes that have emerged. Persons and groups are often surprised by the impressions they make and leave on folks on the other side of an issue.

• Form a problem-solving task force. A small group of persons with different perspectives can provide several services to the larger group of antagonists. They can define the problem for the group to wrestle with. They can state that problem positively rather than our usual tendency to describe conflicts in negative terms. They can list actions to be taken, brainstorm alternative courses of action, suggest the persons responsible for actions, determine deadlines for action, propose the limits of responsibility, and recommend the outcomes hoped for. They can even be charged with proposing a solution or developing a strategy for resolving the issue. Finally, they may serve as a monitoring group during implementation phases and an evaluative body to appraise the final result of the overall group's work.

• Establish a common data base. All parties involved in the difference of opinion can list the undisputed facts in the situation. This listing of a few or many commonly agreed on facts provides a foundation for mutual problem-solving. Sometimes polarized groups forget that they still agree on some issues. These agreements, when discovered, named, and owned, can change the climate of the group from negative to positive.

• Negotiate openly. Good faith negotiating means we exchange ideas with the intention of agreement. Too much bargaining in our competitive society is done with an "I win–you lose" attitude. An effective new method called "principled negotiation" spotlights four principles that offer a baseline for agreement.[2] (1) Separate the people from the problem. (2) Focus on interests, not positions. (3) Invent options for mutual gain. (4) Insist on using objective criteria. These methods reduce the tendency toward win-lose solutions and the temptation to use dirty tactics. Win-win resolutions are more likely when open negotiation becomes the approach in group problem-solving.

• Depersonalize issues. Describe issues in terms of their content and merits rather than blaming and attaching them to their sponsors. This approach helps lessen the probability of issues deteriorating into personality conflicts.

• Use consensus as your decision-making method. Voting—even when the search is for majority opinion—divides groups. A group that is already focusing on its differences may not be able to tolerate additional divisions. Moreover, a vote often pushes subgroups to form coalitions with other persons who hold similar positions or even with opponents in order to "win" the day. A slight majority vote may also "settle" an issue but leave the group unable to move ahead because of the thin mandate of a marginal vote. Consensus means a strong, clear agreement; it doesn't imply or require unanimity. Consensus usually emerges slowly and calls on leaders to listen carefully for "the sense of the body." In principle, patience pays off when parties are collaborating and moving toward consensus.

• *Settle for the "salami technique."* Negotiations tend to move slowly and unevenly. Sometimes more successful negotiators avoid asking for the whole package. Rather, they request one thin slice, get an accommodation, and then ask for another tiny slice. Using this patient but persistent pattern, they may end up with the whole salami. This style of negotiating recognizes that most of us establish our outer limits of compromise more clearly than our nearer limits.

• Brainstorm new alternatives. Even promising negotiations can use a range of possible solutions.

Coping with Emotional Conflicts

A range of actions also forms a structure for resolving feeling-oriented conflicts. No special sequence is intended in the following suggestions.

• Assure a safe climate for taking the risk of sharing personal perspectives. Evenhanded leadership, confidential handling of privately shared information, and building personal and organizational confidence by developing a positive self-image for the congregation are all healthy climate builders.

• Use structured settings to help control anger, frustration, and other emotions. A defined process lends limits for examining potentially explosive feelings.

• Use active listening techniques and well-timed feedback. These communication approaches recognize feelings and clarify their impacts on others.

• Structure some discussion sessions without any decision-making activities on the agenda. Since there is no pressure to settle the divisive concerns immediately, people are more comfortable in opening up with their own emotions and in looking for resolution possibilities for the group. Rational exploration can reduce the emotional level of peacemaking.

• Arrange conversations with antagonists designed to allow them to blow off some steam. These sessions can be either individual conversations or small group discussions (or both). In some conflicts, folks mainly want to be heard. If their need to be taken seriously can be dealt with behind the scenes, the larger congregation may be spared some discomfort.

A Tool Kit for Conflicts About Feelings

A number of conflict management approaches can be utilized in coping with disagreements that take on an emotional flavor or deteriorate into personality clashes. This list is random and is intended to give options to peacemakers.

• Agree on communication rules. Here's one way structure can become an ally in messy conflicts. Consider these "rules." (1) Speak only for yourself. Urge participants to represent their own points of view only. Ask all to share their ideas. If someone chooses not to speak up, let them know that they've allowed their perspective to be unheard and their insights to be unknown. (2) Speak one at a time. This guideline both encourages better listening and slows down the pace of communication, and, therefore, conflict. (3) Speak to specific others. If the actions or views of someone in the group are being discussed, ask for that person to be addressed directly. In that manner, incorrect information or impressions can be clarified immediately. Furthermore, persons are held accountable for their behaviors. (4) Describe behaviors only. Motives and values are difficult to call into question. Don't try. Limit discussion to overt actions and explore the impact of these behaviors.
• Use the Rogerian repetition technique. This approach is a carryover from nondirective counseling. It requires a speaker to sum up the previous speaker's statements to the satisfaction of the previous speaker before adding to or rebutting the earlier ideas.
• Don't allow volume or rage to hijack the congregation's

mission. Some fighters deliberately use bluff, bluster, and confrontive tactics to intimidate leaders and groups into giving in to them. Brace yourself against being overwhelmed or confused by dirty fighters.

• Use a circular seating arrangement. This approach fits most conflict management situations. However, when the conflict in question is an emotional one, even how a group is arranged during problem-solving sessions becomes important. Working in a circle somewhat reduces the "My side of the aisle is against your side of the aisle" feeling that other configurations may imply.

• Reserve the right to call a "time out." When emotions overflow, the leader can take the initiative to call a recess in order to let emotions cool a bit. One variation on this method is "stopping the music" by freezing discussion at a point in time and immediately evaluating the process and progress to this stage.

• Adopt a double column method of evaluating potential solutions. When some resolution options emerge, ask the group to appraise them using two columns, one for favorable factors in the suggestion and the other for questionable factors. This method is intended to cut down on only advocating or simply rejecting a possible solution by involving all in looking at both sides of the idea.

• Pull the plug and encourage everyone to say what's on their minds. This step, while risky and requiring good leadership, can unblock the emotions that may be hampering the process.

• Help those who are defeated save face. In spite of the fact that effective peacemakers strive for win-win resolutions, sometimes persons lose or at least feel they have lost. Their self-esteem deserves to be preserved. Don't rub losers' noses in their loss if your relationship to them is important to you.

Facing Your Own Anger

Leaders aren't always neutral peacemakers. Sometimes they can cause conflict too. Leaders' anger can overflow and create havoc. Laurence Peter notes, "Speak when you're angry—and you'll make the best speech you'll ever regret." Understanding and facing personal anger is, therefore, a crucial factor in leaderhip.[3]

Broadly speaking, we face conflict with one of two responses—either we fight or we take flight. If we fight, we cope with conflicts confrontively, directly, and overtly. If we take flight, we cope with conflicts passively, indirectly, and covertly. However, the spectrum of reactions to anger that falls between fight and flight offers several variations on the two themes.

Fight————————————————————— Flight

> Angry/Outspoken
> Angry/Manipulative
> Angry/Afraid
> Angry/Depressed
> Angry/Immobilized
> Angry/Withdrawn

Illustration 23. Anger Spectrum

• When leaders are *angry and outspoken,* they act like the biblical "sons of thunder" (Mark 3:17). Their overt expressions of anger create distance from others. They may find their sense of timing ruined if they develop a short fuse and explode randomly. However, because they feel their anger near the surface, they may also be able to deal with their anger openly, candidly, and honestly.

• When leaders are *angry and manipulative,* they may be more disguised with their real feelings. If so, they may do an "end run" and make negative comments about opponents or spread rumors or engage in congregational politics. They may convey their disaffection indirectly and use veiled communication, like sarcasm, to convey their resentment or sense of competition.

• When leaders are *angry and afraid,* they may panic and feel a sense of helplessness welling up inside. They may become too dependent on others for approval and support. Worse yet, they may become emotionally paralyzed and unable to take responsible action.

• When leaders are *angry and depressed,* they turn their anger inward and become blue, lackadaisical, and inert. They may feel it's preferable to be depressed than to be openly angry.

• When leaders are *angry and immobilized,* they are choosing to survive by anesthetizing their feelings. They develop a protective veneer over their emotions and fade out rather than dissent. Apathy, inactivity, and lack of concern disguise their resentment because their anger has gone unnoticed.

• When leaders are *angry and withdrawn,* they use distance to cope with their negative feelings. They may pull back from groups in conflict or even leave one congregation for another. "Circuit rider" leaders who repeatedly move from church to church may resist buying into new groups and protect themselves by exiting group after group when conflict arises.

"Know thyself," instructed Socrates. This advice applies doubly for church leaders and our anger. How we express our own conflicts is a key ingredient in the conregational leadership mix.

Overview: Conflict Resolution

Conflict pits persons against one another in competitive stances. For descriptive purposes, congregational conflict can be categorized as fact-based or feeling-oriented. Factual differences can often be negotiated. Emotional conflicts usually require ventilation. Both approaches can be implemented with a variety of methods. Individually, leaders need to be clear about how they face anger and conflict.

Review Questions

1 What is conflict?
2. What are two basic types of conflict?
3. What methods apply best to resolving factual and feeling conflicts?

Notes

1. Two helpful books on conflict management methods are Speed Leas and Paul Kittlaus, *Church Fights: Managing Conflict in the Local Church* (Philadelphia: Westminster Press, 1973) and Larry L. McSwain and William C. Treadwell, Jr., *Conflict Ministry in the Church* (Nashville: Broadman Press, 1981).
2. Roger Fisher and William Ury, *Getting to Yes: Negotiating Agreement Without Giving In* (New York: Penguin Books, 1981).
3. Daniel B. Bagby, *Understanding Anger in the Church* (Nashville: Broadman Press, 1979).

A Selected Bibliography on Conflict Resolution

Bagby, Daniel G. *Understanding Anger in the Church.* Nashville: Broadman Press, 1979.

Fisher, Roger, and Ury, William. *Getting to Yes: Negotiating Agreement Without Giving In.* New York: Penguin Books, 1981.

Leas, Speed, and Kittlaus, Paul. *Church Fights: Managing Conflict in the Local Church.* Philadelphia: Westminster Press, 1973.

Lewis, G. Douglas. *Resolving Church Conflicts: A Case Study Approach for Local Congregations.* New York: Harper & Row, 1981.

McSwain, Larry L., and Treadwell, William C., Jr. *Conflict Ministry in the Church.* Nashville: Broadman Press, 1981.

Pnewman, Roy W., and Bruehl, Margaret E. *Managing Conflict: A Complete Process-Centered Handbook.* Englewood Cliffs, N.J.: Prentice-Hall, 1982.

— 14 —

HANDLING TRANSITIONS BETWEEN MINISTRY POSTS

HELLO AND GOOD-BYE are crucial words for leadership in ministry. The transitions of ministry start-up and ministry closure are pivotal processes. Both set the atmosphere for effective ministry. Both are intensely personal expressions of ministry. Both are often taken for granted.

"I made some mistakes during start-up that plagued me for the entire eleven years of my ministry there. I'm wiser about start-up now and hope I won't repeat my past errors here," stated a new Missouri pastor. A young Methodist pastor noted, "I must understand the possibilities and perils of start-up. I'll probably repeat the start-up process seven or eight times during my ministry." Ministers who serve in denominations with a call system (as opposed to an appointive system) may spend as much as 30 to 50 percent of their overall ministries doing start-up work.

Ministry start-up generally refers to the first twelve to eighteen months of establishing the relationships and roles for effective ministry in a new post. Looking at start-up deliberately is a recent phenomenon.

Ministry start-up is pivotal. Not only does start-up set the tone for later ministry, it can also become the occasion for several ministerial sins.

(1) Start-up can open ministers to the sin of discontinuity. New ministers may act as if redemptive history only begins with their entry into that church. The sin of

discontinuity ignores the "cloud of witnesses" (Heb. 12:1) in the stream of Christianity who have been faithful to God long before we came along. Blindness to continuity may encourage us to feel that what's new to us is also new to God and his people.

(2) Start-up can trigger the sin of destiny. This sin tempts new ministers to act as if they stand at the center of history themselves. Every generation has the tendency to think it is living at the hinge of history—the ones who will change the direction of civilization. When new ministers' sense of their place in the eternal plan of God becomes overblown, they may assume they, rather than Christ, stand at the center of things.

(3) Start-up also creates the atmosphere for the sin of professionalism. New ministers may act as if they alone have the vision of God, the only ones who see the end of history clearly. Obviously, a view of the kingdom of God is essential for effective ministers. But, to exclude other individual or congregational visions of the kingdom is to commit the sin of professionalism. Assuming that only we who are ordained have the insight or skill to advance God's kingdom is dangerous.

The Dynamics of the Interim Period

The interim period, the vacancy between pastors experienced by churches using the call method for securing ministers, contains some interesting dynamics. Whether the former minister has resigned, been fired, or has died, the time of searching for a new minister is a strategic interval for several congregational processes.

• *Grief occurs.* Loss is an overarching issue during interims. Grief is painful and triggers a variety of responses in congregations. The ways Jesus' followers faced their grief over the loss of their leader illustrate the point. One response is denial. It sets off the "good old what's his name" reaction. Simon Peter's anger and cursing at the campfire after Jesus' arrest (Luke 22:54-62) illustrate this reflex. Judas's reaction demonstrates how guilt arises from grief (Matt. 27:3-5). Additionally, among the persons who witnessed the crucifixion, shock and helplessness created a "Stop the world—I want to get off" response (Luke 23:50-53).

I was once a lay member of a church when our pastor resigned. He had served the church very effectively for an extended tenure. Although he guided the good-bye saying process rather skillfully, the congregation suffered considerable grief. Three or four weeks into the interim we held an election to choose key lay leaders. A strange attitude surfaced. The vote was light. Many of the persons who received strong support declined to serve. The overall response was so uncharacteristically poor that a congregational meeting was called to discuss the reasons. Our conclusion was simple: the congregation was still so mired in grief that effective decision-making was unlikely. We decided to set the election aside, concentrate on working through our loss, and then face our leadership decisions a bit later. In a few weeks another election was held, and this time the vote was heavy and the members who garnered strong support gladly agreed to serve. The lesson is obvious. Without effective grief work during the interim period, the work of ministry is hampered.

• *Leaders fade and emerge.* Power is another key issue during interims. Congregational leaders tend to agree with their pastor. When the minister leaves, however, a new situation develops. Some leaders who have been waiting on the sidelines now move into the mainstream of the church's decision-making. Others who have been extremely active may choose the interim and beyond for a sabbatic leave from leadership responsibilities.

One dynamic that encourages the ebb and flow of lay leadership during interims as the practice of selecting a broadly representative search committee. Normally, congregations select women and men of differing ages and perspectives to serve in the search process. This approach automatically stirs the leadership mix in the church and redistributes power.

• *The relationship between a congregation and its denomination is clarified.* A ministerial vacancy usually reduces the congregation's channels of access to its larger denominational resources. The relational ties between a congregation and its denomination are still vital. The relationship ranges from control to assistance. Some churches demonstrate dependency toward their denominational resources by begging for direction. Other congregations show counter-dependence and reject any denominational help that's available or offered. Frequently, interdependence and shared resources are discovered and carried forward into the next chapter of ministry. Whichever relationship is developed, the links of trust or distrust between local congregations and regional or national denomination groups are generally expanded during interims.

• *Congregational mission is explored.* The most common process during interims is clarifying identity. The minister's exit often creates an identity gap because the minister is the spokesperson or the publicist for the congregation's dream. Who are we? Where are we headed as a fellowship? These basic questions redefine the congregation's vision.

During a vacancy consultation, a denominational leader kept hearing two themes emerging from conversations with the congregation of a stable, suburban church. "We want a young, energetic minister who can draw young people back into our church" was counterbalanced with the statement, "We have lots of widows and widowers in our church." Finally, the consultant raised a question, "Exactly how many widows and widowers are 'lots'?" After a survey, the church discovered it had 154 widowed members. That was an important fact. It turned the pastoral search toward more mature prospective ministers. A pastor in his fifties was called; the congregation now points to the consultant's question as a significant step in identifying its internal mission.

Loss, power, denominational links, and identity—these basic issues surface regularly during interim periods. How well or how poorly these concerns are dealt with provides a backdrop for the new minister's start-up work.

Start-up Stoppers

Getting off to a good start is crucial in ministry, as in many other ministry activities. Some events or processes can become barriers to effective ministry start-up. Here's a checklist of a variety of "stoppers."[1] While the checklist of possible happenings noted below has no predictable sequence of occurrence, an attempt has been made to place them in order of likelihood.

• *Congregations and other ministry agencies typically take better care of your physical needs than your spiritual ones during the settling in process.* The transition from one ministry post to another is difficult for both minister and congregation. The transition differs, however, for these two parties. For the congregation, the new minister's arrival marks the end of an interim period. The congregation feels some relief that the uncertainty of the interim is over. The added security and structure personified in the minister is comforting. The attitude of the congregation is usually: "Welcome. We're glad you're here. Now, let's get down to business as usual." The congregation concentrates on getting the minister moved into the parsonage or home, helps fill the refrigerator and pantry, and then returns to their normal activities. In some ways settling the minister in is similar to the congregation's response to a funeral. That is, when a fellow church member dies, the congregation rallies around with casseroles, sympathy cards, and expressions of support. They take off time from work to attend the funeral. And then they return to their usual routines (while the bereaved family begins its longer-term grief process). The congregation moves from intense involvement with survivors to virtual abandonment of the grieving survivors. Likewise, when the new minister moves onto the church field, the congregation often retreats in relief to normal activity patterns.

For the minister, settling into a new ministry post marks a beginning. More than just a new job opportunity, leading a new congregation requires taking risks and establishing relationships. It begins a monumental process full of possibilities and anxieties. Attention is needed both to the immediate physical adjustments of settling into a new living setting as well as to the longer-term spiritual and emotional needs of the minister.

• *Ministers often fall into a rescuer mode and attempt a "quick fix" approach when congregational confidence has eroded.* The exit of the former minister coupled with the interim period, if not dealt with well, can weaken the congregation's self-estimate. Likewise, feelings about leaving the former place of service and the natural uncertainties arising out of entering a new congregational relationship can trigger self-questioning by the minister. Doubting congregations may cry out to be rescued and settle into a dependent relationship with the new minister that blocks partnership in ministry. Doubting ministers may either bend over backwards in an attempt to please everyone or move too quickly to apply an old reliable program to the new situation even if it doesn't fit or isn't needed.

• *First impressions are tricky.* First impressions are based on very selective information with few exposures to the minister. They often become permanent impressions. Many first impressions are formed during the first worship service the minister leads, more during the first week of the minister's work, and most by the end of the first month.

The criteria for judging a minister during an initial encounter vary. Several years ago a friend of mine was to preach a candidate sermon at a pastorless church. The airline lost his luggage. He arrived in an unfamiliar city late on Saturday afternoon without a change of clothes or his Bible containing his sermon notes. A quick trip to

J. C. Penney's supplied a fresh shirt; using the Gideon Bible from his motel room, he memorized his sermon text. The next morning the visiting pracher felt the service went well—but the congregation turned him down. Why? Because (1) he wore a colored shirt (rather than the expected white one), (2) he didn't use the Bible (in spite of the fact that he quoted his text from memory), and (3) he used no preaching notes (supposedly indicating that he wasn't carefully prepared). All three "reasons" for not calling the guest preacher were based on highly subjective first-impression data.

Essentially, the individualistic expectations persons use for first-impression criteria revolve around items like using familiar words and phrases, smiling, and remembering members' names. These criteria boil down to two questions: "Are you real?" and "Do you care?"

• *History must be taken seriously.* The past generally propels the congregation toward its future. Most congregations supply prospective ministers with statistical data about their program organizations and sociological information about their communities. While this type of information is broadly helpful, it doesn't tell the congregation's deeper history.

It's important for new ministers to discover the "sacred" stories, events, and objects early in their start-up processes. A friend of mine accidentally marched into a historical minefield. He found the new church's fellowship hall had a clock that no longer worked hanging on its back wall. After fretting about the useless clock for a brief period of time, he removed the clock from its place. To his surprise, the clock's removal created a fuss. Why the reaction? Because a prominent church family had given the clock years before. Everyone knew the clock didn't work, but they considered it an heirloom and an important memory of the contributions of a key family in their fellowship. Inadvertently, the new pastor had disturbed a symbol of the congregation's history.

Like Joshua's recounting of Israel's history in Joshua

24:1-27, new ministers can ask some lifelong member of the congregation to overview the church's past informally or structure a group of laypersons to interpret the history of the body. Such a consciousness-raising project may prevent new ministers from the accidental arrogance of acting as if nothing of real importance has happened in this church prior to their arrival.

• *The "ghosts of pastors past" shape how the congregation will value and treat its new minister.* The new minister in a church often hears the "war stories" about the former minister. When the stories are laudatory, the new minister must resist the feeling of threat by comparison. When the stories are complaints, the new minister must squelch the impulse to join in judgmental gripes. However, talking about the former minister allows the natural grief process to run its course.

Is it easier to follow a successful minister or one who was a failure for some reason? Contrary to popular wisdom, it's probably easier to succeed a predecessor who did well. To use financial metaphors, "borrowed credit," or the good feelings church members attach to the former minister or ministers, accrue to the new minister. On the other hand, "inherited debt," or the distrust related to bad experiences with former ministers, is also attached to the new minister's start-up work. When laypersons have felt used and abused or lied to and disappointed, the new minister faces the considerable task of re-establishing the confidence of the laity in ministers.

• *Poor stewardship of the "honeymoon" transition dampens early momentum.* Congregations don't know what the new minister knows (and doesn't know) or can do (or can't do). They generally allow lots of room and latitude. This extra space causes a suspension of judgment that creates the "transition energy" commonly called the "honeymoon."

Laypersons often offer the new minister an almost endless supply of blank checks. (Remember the "almost.") These free "yeses" can be seductive. New ministers can become so intoxicated by the momentum of the honeymoon that they squander the positive feelings of the honeymoon on secondary issues or projects.

One misappropriation of transition energy can be caused by the new minister's anxiety. A common reaction to new situations is "nest making" activity designed to calm the uncertainties of start-up. Ministers may make themselves comfortable with familiar programs or routines at the expense of the congregation's excitement about having a new pastoral leader.

• *Expect to be tested (but not necessarily confronted).* Many new ministers either don't expect to be tested or don't recognize tests when they occur. Laity do, however, check their new ministers out. The kinds of hidden questions raised of new ministers vary widely.

Some new ministers miss seeing their test cases because of what they think of as a "suspended judgment" quality of the honeymoon. Apparently, there's a two-tiered structure to the honeymoon. First, there's a "pedestal phase" of a month or so when the congregation and new minister relate to each other on the basis of almost no meaningful information. Typically, new objects are overvalued—new babies, new cars, new spouses, and new ministers. This stage can become so intoxicating that perspective is easy to lose. But, after a while, the new wears off. Then the second stage, the "wait and see phase," begins. During this time people withhold feedback and act as if everything is going well—even if they think it isn't. New ministers may lose the confidence of their church members during this stage and not even realize when or how the breach occurred.

Ministers test their new congregations too. The end result of the testing from both sides is a growing sense of mutual knowledge and a more realistic relationship.

• *The honeymoon will end; don't let it end you.* At some point in time determined by an intuitive clock, the honeymoon ends. Minister and congregation now know each other, and reality sets in. When heavier information and emotions begin to be shared, it's a frightening time. Either a new and more mature understanding for ministry can be negotiated, or the emerging ministry relationship may end prematurely. A growing number of ministers are building a regular review and re-negotiation process into the early portion of their ministry start-up. This structure helps new ministers update their relationship with the congregation.

• *The first conflict in a new church sets the tone for dealing with differences during later ministry there.* An acquaintance of mine claims his honeymoon in a new church lasted until noon on the first day of his ministry work. As soon as his moving van arrived, a church member came by to help unload it. Instead, the member "unloaded" his views of another church member. By noon the first member had finished his complaints and gone. Almost immediately the member whose character and motives had just been questioned arrived. He began to vent his anger at the first member. The new pastor noted that by noon of his first day on the new church field he knew he was in the middle of a conflict that hadn't been settled during the interim period. His honeymoon in that church lasted only about two hours!

It isn't uncommon for churches to experience the "Wait until your father gets home" syndrome. That condition occurs when a simmering conflict brewing just below the surface of the congregation is exposed as soon as the new minister arrives. If these conflicts haven't been or can't be dealt with during the interim, a third party may be needed to help the church deal with its differences and to keep the new pastor's ministry intact.

The way the first conflict is faced sets the tone and often determines the techniques later conflicts will use. When trust between parties hasn't had time to develop, conflicts are especially difficult to resolve.

• *Expect the power structure in new pastorates to change (and this change may vary from a small one to a drastic one).* Generally, the interim period triggers a shift in the power structure in the church. Inactive members may reassert themselves; overactive members may cut back on their involvement. The power adjustment process continues after the new minister arrives. The leadership corps of the church typically consists of roughly 20 percent of the congregation. These leaders are ordinarily compatible with the minister's theology, work patterns, age, and life style. The new minister's approach may attract members from the 80 percent of those who are less involved into the leadership circle. By the same token, old leaders may recede into the background if they feel uncomfortable with the new minister.

• *Surprises aren't necessarily destructive during new ministry start-up.* One way to track unanticipated events or unfulfilled expectations during start-up is to write down surprises. Since so many new faces, experiences, and impressions are swirling around in the new minister's head during start-up anyway, it's easy to lose perspective on what's occurring in the start-up process. Surprises are those events and perceptions that don't match expectations. They jump out at the new leader. Note them and monitor what's happening in the process.

• *Early change efforts should be selected deliberately.* Change in many churches is a slow process. The momentum of the honeymoon period lures some new pastors into making lots of changes early. Too frequently these changes are ill advised.

Early change efforts can convey the impression to the laity that the new pastor thinks they didn't know how to worship or make decisions or "do church" with the old minister. Hasty changes also suggest to laypersons that the new minister has a pre-determined agenda and won't listen to their needs.

There isn't any magic time before which changes aren't wise or after which changes are automatically legitimate. Changes that are needed by the congregation, wanted by the congregation, and supported by the congregation are timely regardless of whether the minister is new or not.

• *Denominations are generally in the new minister's corner—and they expect the new pastor to make good things happen soon.* Denominations often treat new ministers very much like the congregation itself does—they rally around until the minister is settled, and then they pull back. The expectation that the new minister will be cooperative and productive doesn't go away, though.

• *Mismatches with the former minister's leader style may strain start-up efforts.* A comfortable leader style–follower style mesh usually develops over time. Whenever a specific comfort level emerges, a kind of corporate expectation about the minister's leader style develops. If the new minister expresses a different amount of initiative or a different quality of authority, discomfort is felt by the congregation. If the new minister's leader style doesn't exert as much initiative as the former minister's did, a gap is produced, and projects fall between the cracks and are left undone. Frustration bubbles up. On the other hand, if the new minister uses lots more initiative than the congregation became comfortable with during the former minister's tenure, the minister and laypersons find themselves overlapping into one another's traditional territory. Conflict is likely.

Since effective leaders relate comfortably with their followers, style mismatches must be confronted. When the leader and followers are out of sync, who changes? Hopefully, both can adjust over time. During start-up, however, the new minister can usually adjust more easily than the group. As a practical matter, one person can bend more easily than an entire congregation.

Start-up Strategies

A deliberate approach to getting acquainted and established is crucial for ministers. These start-up strategies guide the new minister's priorities and provide structure for actions.

- *Begin with people and build sturdy relationships.* Launching ministry with a "names and needs" philosophy is a sound approach. Concentrating on getting acquainted with members and prospective members through home visits and other planned contacts provides the foundation for your future ministry. Three resources emerge from relationship-building efforts: (1) we discover our most comfortable ministry role, (2) we gain basic information for ministry, and (3) we gather personal and professional support for ministry.
- *Help the congregation define its ministry dream.* Nothing is more basic to ministry success than discovering what the congregation senses God wants from it here and now. Scan chapters 6 and 7 on diagnosing congregational climate and sharpening vision for suggestions about awakening a ministry dream.
- *Preach and teach mainstream issues and create a warm climate during worship.* Stick to familiar terrain in the selection of preaching and teaching materials during start-up. While the content of early sermons and teaching presentations is important, the tone of your public statements may be even more crucial in establishing a heart-bond with members. Most beginning ministers prefer to focus on affirming, joyous, warm, lighter, and more folksy attitudes that encourage self-identification with others.
- *Search for real needs.* Any congregational or community need that hasn't been taken seriously is a potent ministry and programming possibility. Vacuum areas generally receive strong and immediate responses.
- *Cultivate healthy congregational habits.* Organizations develop habitual methods, called norms, for doing their work. "The way things are done here" can be healthy and growth inducing or unhealthy and growth stunting. Establish positive norms around your early ministry. "I intend to be the pastor of every member" and "My door is open to you" and "Tell me about the hospitalized and burdened persons who need a visit" are examples of

healthy pastoral norms. These kinds of habits can be extended to the congregation at large.

• *Don't forget the needs of your family and yourself.* Ask more questions. Toss more footballs. Go on more picnics. Otherwise, beware of the results—physically, spiritually, and emotionally—of "all work and no play."

Covenants for Start-up

Two different kinds of arrangements aid ministers during start-up: support groups and installation services. Support groups are available in several types. Some minister's support groups are structured by denominations to provide encouragement for their ministers; other support groups are ecumenical gatherings of community ministers. Increasingly, congregations are naming standing pastoral relations committees or asking their pastoral search committees to remain intact to provide encouragement and feedback to the new minister during start-up and beyond.

Installation services are also becoming more popular and practical. The flavor of an installation service should be more like a wedding than a personnel process. The minister and congregation solemnly consider their roles and responsibilities. Then they pledge to work together. These special services of affirmation are ordinarily led by the interim pastor or a denominational leader. The vows exchanged during the installation service can be renewed on anniversaries of the minister's call or at special events like homecoming or renewal services.

Closure: Saying Good-bye Constructively

Closure—closing out a ministry in a particular place—is also an important leadership concern. Your congregation's official documents or your denomination's guidelines may specify how you resign. But these formal materials don't determine how you will leave. How you leave a ministry post flavors how your ministry is seen and evaluated. Closure either makes your good ministry better or the bad even worse.

You have the initiative in the manner of closing out your ministry. Take into account several dimensions of the art and science of saying good-bye to a church. Here's a checklist:

Pastoral Care During Closure

This section begins with pastoral care issues because closure is so relational.
• Leaking information about your resignation and exit creates the appearance of favoritism.
• Be prepared for supporters to react to your exit with pain and, perhaps, rejection.
• Guard against putdowns by comparison. Your natural enthusiasm about new opportunities may imply that the current setting for ministry is somehow inferior.
• Deal directly with persons with special needs. Give maximum support to counselees and complete referral arrangements. Work with elderly members who may have included you in their funeral plans. Encourage the spiritual growth of converts and new members. Assure the children of your congregation that your exit isn't a rejection of them. Be prepared for some previously antagonistic members to move closer to you.

Pastoral Management During Closure

A variety of management actions can ease the closure process.
• The impact of your leadership style will surface during your exit process. If you've created a sense of congregational dependency, get ready for panic. If you've helped lay leaders mature and have developed a solid administrative structure, the congregation is more likely to proceed with some degree of confidence.
• You're a lame duck. That means you have much less formal power. So don't attempt wholesale changes now. Offer assistance and tie up loose ends.

- Leave a transition packet of legal and administrative documents in one place for your successor.
- If your relationships will allow it, help formulate some administrative guidelines for the interim period. These clarifications assure the stability of the organization.
- If your relationships will allow it, you may want to offer to do an exit interview in the style of business and industry.

Pastoral Preaching During Closure

Since preaching is such a public ministry, the themes you choose and the mood you exhibit are vital.

- Don't use your final sermon to say everything you've always wanted to say to this congregation before but were afraid to try—especially if you're angry.
- Proclaim the basic mission of the church. A sense of vision gives the congregation additional direction and structure for the interim.
- Announce your future relationship to the congregation. If return-to-the-field ethics aren't handled well, even good ministries can be spoiled. If you're planning to be available for weddings or funerals, specify the conditions and at whose invitation you'd consider returning to the field to conduct services.
- You may want to deliver a state-of-the-church address noting progress and thanking people for their faithfulness. Challenge them to future service. This message may amount to a public exit interview.
- Consider a service of termination—the opposite of an installation—in a congregational setting.

P.S.—Don't Forget Yourself

Closure has several personal dimensions too. Handle the losses you and your family will face by talking about them, by staying physically active, and by planning your move carefully. Expect to be blue. Keep your devotional disciplines current. Prepare for the new workplace by subscribing to a local newspaper. Get ready to take initiative in building a new personal and professional support system. Ministers have a huge advantage in closure and start-up over other professionals—a built-in community. Let your new church reach out and care for you. You'll need the encouragement—and, if you do your work well, you'll repay your membership in service many fold.

Overview: Handling Ministry Transitions

Ministry start-up and ministry closure are crucial transitions in effective leadership. Either we guide these two processes constructively, or we pay high prices in lower congregational morale because of our ineptitude. These transitions involve personal as well as professional dimensions.

Review Questions

1. What are the primary dynamics of the interim period between ministers?
2. What are some likely happenings during ministry start-up that can hinder effective work?
3. What are some start-up strategies?
4. How can ministry closure be handled effectively?

Notes

1. The research for this checklist is drawn extensively from Roy M. Oswald, *The Pastor as Newcomer* (Washington, D.C.: Alban Institute, 1977).

Selected Bibliography on Ministry Start-up and Closure

Feinberg, Mortimer R.; Feinberg, Floria; and Tarrant, John J. *Leavetaking.* New York: Simon & Schuster, 1978.
Grubbs, Bruce. *The First Two Years: A Pastor's Guide to Getting Started in a Church.* Nashville: Convention Press, 1979.

Hahn, Celia A. *The Minister Is Leaving.* New York: Seabury Press, n.d.

Kemper, Robert. *Beginning a New Pastorate.* Nashville: Abingdon Press, 1978.

Oswald, Roy M. *New Beginnings: Pastorate Start Up Notebook.* Washington, D.C.: Alban Institute, 1977.

———. *Running Through the Thistles: Terminating a Ministerial Relationship with a Parish.* Washington, D.C.: Alban Institute, 1977.

Schaller, Lyle E. *The Pastor and the People.* Nashville: Abingdon Press, 1973.

IV.
Exploring Personal Dimensions of Leadership: An Overview

— 15 —

SPIRITUAL DISCIPLINES
FOR LEADERS

EFFECTIVE LEADERS RECOGNIZE a center, a pivot, for our lives. In religious vocations, that life priority customarily pivots on the fulcrum of spiritual disciplines. After all, for the leader who envisions the kingdom of God, what better core value to emphasize than the spiritual life? As Jesus taught, we who follow him are to "seek first his kingdom" (Matt. 6:33).

Drawing the Target

Think of the priorities of our lives as a target made up of a bull's-eye and several larger concentric circles expanding out from the central core. The bull's-eye represents our highest priority—the leader's spiritual life. After all, nothing is more critical to pastoral leaders than our healthy relationship to Christ. No other "success" in ministry is meaningful if we lose the vitality of our life in Christ. Remember Christ's question about the ultimate profit-loss statement? He asked, "For what does it profit a man, to gain the whole world and forfeit his life?" (Mark 8:36). Wealth or prominence, for example, is a high price to pay if it costs us our best selves.

Picture the spiritual target like this.[1]
Listed below are several guidelines that grow out of this model of priorities in ministry. Note that these guidelines

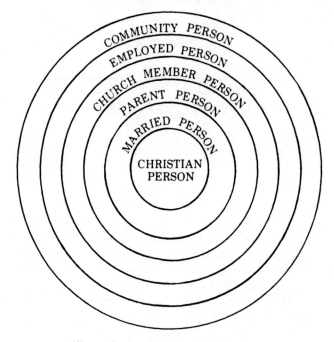

Illustration 24. Ministry Priorities Model

are stated in terms of *if*. *If* is that little, but crucial, word reminding us that success in ministry is often based on *if* or *on the condition that*. After all, our values and decisions naturally have consequences. *If* implies a *then*. Consider these priority *if's* and their impact on our spiritual lives and ministries.

• If we are clear about our personal and professional goals, then the inner circle controls all other priorities. In other words, priorities are set from the inside out on this model. The pulls of the outer circles shouldn't disengage us from the push or spiritual propulsion of the bull's-eye itself.
• If the innermost circle is weak or neglected, then the lesser priorities represented by the other circles are also

undermined. The life of the Spirit provides a foundation for empowering all our ministry efforts.

● If one of the outer circles is given priority over one of the inner circles, or worse yet, the bull's-eye itself, then ministry is undercut. In this case, we have probably confused the important with the essential. One of the most difficult aspects of setting ministry priorities is that we are constantly making the tricky choices between the good and the best.

● If the order of priorities suggested by the model is upheld, then effectiveness and satisfaction in ministry are more likely to result. A clear decision about our values and precedents makes success in ministry a higher possibility. Again, the crux of our priority structure is the vitality of our relationship with Christ as Savior and Lord.

Where do leaders turn for strength and vision? A variety of answers is possible, but Elizabeth O'Connor's observation is fundamental for quality leadership.

> We are not called primarily to create new structures for the church in this age; we are not called primarily to a program of service, or to dream dreams or have visions. We are called first of all to belong to Jesus Christ as Savior and Lord, and to keep our lives warmed at the hearth of His life. It is there the fire will be lit which will create new structures and programs of service that will draw others into the circle to dream and have visions.
>
> To understand this is to be thrown back upon those disciplines which are the only known gateways to the grace of God; for how do we fulfill the command to love, except that we learn it of God, and how do we learn it of God, except that we pray, and live under His Word and perceive His world?[2]

Cataloging Devotional Options

Religious leaders have and use a wide range of resources and materials to deepen our spiritual lives.[3] Our sense of the holy in our lives keeps us from callously treating our vision of the kingdom of God as a possession and a leadership lever instead of spiritual empowerment. Note the catalog of some possibilities listed below. Blend them into a regular, but flexible, pattern to nourish inner life.

• *Use meditative Bible reading.* Pastoral leaders have many opportunities to read and study the Bible. Sermon texts must be selected and exegeted; Bible studies and devotionals must be prepared. If ministers don't guard against it, however, we may find ourselves reading the Bible for others' instruction only rather than for our own nurture and renewal too. Meditation is the listening side of prayer. As such, meditating on the Bible offers us vital refreshment.

Meditative Bible reading allows us to read passages leisurely and thoughtfully. We can explore the mood as well as the meaning of the section of the Bible under consideration. We may focus on a paragraph or chapter of scripture and deliberately let the passage soak into our lives and minds. Psalm 1 and Psalm 23 are prime passages to read meditatively. Or, we may project ourselves into a Bible story. For example, we might read an event from Christ's life, such as the Gethsemane experience (Matt. 26:36-46), and live out the scene in our imaginations to see which character we identify with. We can follow our thoughts, images, and sensations as well as any sights or sounds our minds project. We may even choose to analyze our imagings to see if we can discover why these particular thoughts emerged. Keeping a journal or spiritual diary can add a longitudinal dimension to our spiritual growth.

• *Develop the practice of prayer.* Prayer is the active, speaking side of meditation. As such, praise, adoration, petition, and intercession all have their time and place in the practice of prayer. A prayer group may help us add structure, strength, and variety to our use of prayer as a spiritual growth resource.

• *Enlist a spiritual director.* A mature leader with a disciplined devotional life and the gift of sensitivity offers the resource of friendly guidance. More about this approach is discussed in the section exploring a spiritual coach which follows later in this chapter.

• *Read the biographies and letters of great leaders of the Christian movement.* Augustine's *Confessions* and the letters of Martin Luther, John Wesley, Thomas Merton, Frank Laubach, and C. S. Lewis provide insight and inspiration for growth in both spirituality and leadership. For example, Luther once commented that an especially busy day required twice as much time in prayer. That principle offers an important guideline for harried leaders.

• *Read adult parables.* Spiritual truths couched in the form of parable or even fantasy stimulate us to think about our inner lives in new ways. Trina Paulus' popular book *Hope for the Flowers* and Brian Hall's *Nog's Vision* are examples of tales that challenge leaders at the deeper levels of our lives.

• *Read others' prayers.* Sometimes others' prayers expand our own prayer lives. John Baillie's classic volume *A Diary of Private Prayer* provides two daily prayers for a month with a blank page for our own insights. Other helpful materials are also available. To illustrate, Ken Thompson's *Bless This Desk: Prayers from 9 to 5* records some of the devotional expressions of a bivocational minister about his work in the world of advertising. Or, Francis A. Martin's *Prayers from Where You Are* contains spontaneous and sensitive affirmations of faith and is adept at stating universal feeling in prayer form.

• *Read devotional materials.* Denominations provide devotional materials for their members. However, a multitude of free-standing volumes are also available. For instance, William Barclay's books *Daily Celebration* and *In the Hands of God* use biblical reflections and human interest stories to open our minds and hearts to God's challenges. Or, John Baillie's *A Diary of Readings* is designed as an anthology of readings to engage us in serious thought about God each day of the year.

• *Ponder the devotional classics.* Thomas à Kempis' *Imitation of Christ*, William Laws' *A Serious Call*, John

Bunyan's *The Pilgrim's Progress,* and the anonymously authored *The Cloud of Unknowing* inspire readers to explore and deepen our relationship to Christ.

• *Explore the disciplines of denial.* Solitude, silence, fasting, and other forms of self-denial help us learn about ourselves and our inner lives.

• *Reflect on nature.* The sights and sounds of nature provide us an opportunity to sense God in our lives. For example, recently a perceptive friend, who has experienced considerable pain in his life, showed me a plant stalk he had found while walking. The stalk had a bulge almost the size of a golf ball about midway up it. Apparently, an insect had been able to insert an egg inside the stalk when it was small and tender. As the egg grew, the plant's stem had also grown and had compensated for the expanding egg by developing a tough bulb around the egg. My friend noted that most of God's creations are able to thrive in spite of hardships.

• *Face the possibility of the silence of God.* Each of us discovers, to our chagrin, the arid times when our prayers seem to go unanswered. In the Bible, the book of Job illustrates the dilemma well. How can we understand and cope with these silences? Can we be questioned by our own questions while we wait for God's response? Christian therapist Paul Tournier observes helpfully:

> Men throw out questions to God which remain unanswered. But they change, and find unexpected solutions when they begin to listen to the questions God asks them, and to answer them. Jesus did not answer the weighted questions of his contradictors; he always asked them other questions, embarrassing ones, capable of making them take stock of themselves.[4]

Even the silences of God are opportunities to know Him and ourselves better and to learn leadership. Growth emerges from our experiences of weakness as well as strength, from our failures as well as our successes.

Merging Spiritual and Professional Growth

Too many perspectives separate the spiritual disciplines from professional skill growth. Spirituality and leadership can be viewed as two sides of the same coin.[5] For example, planning and praying are both ways to channel energy. Planning focuses our energy toward the future; praying channels God's energy on us and our plans. Or, study and meditative reading match up as we both actively and passively fill ourselves. It's crucial that we view our lives wholistically.

Spirituality and Leader Growth

How can the spiritual disciplines and other elements of a minister's support resources be meshed together for the growth of leaders? Let's consider a wholistic model for integrating leader growth with the basic issue of spiritual development.[6]

The overall model involves five types of growth resources for increasing leaders' personal and professional depth and breadth. Balance and richness in ministry call for all five approaches to be creatively and fairly equally related.

● *The "spiritual coach" resource for devotional health.* Spiritual growth is foundational to leader growth. Spiritual development is an ongoing concern in effective ministry and constructive leadership. Either we grow in Christ, or our faith atrophies. The parable of the talents demonstrates the "use or lose" principle that operates in the stewardship of Christian resources of all types (Matt. 25:14-30). Spiritually, either we grow up, or we shrink up.

In order to grow spiritually, some leaders enlist a spiritual coach. This coach assists in setting and evaluating goals for inner development. Some religious groups have utilized spiritual directors for centuries. The spiritual guide relationship offers one-to-one support. Monitoring our spiritual pilgrimage with the aid of an objective, mature peer is a great advantage for leaders. The disciplines we've already cataloged all have their place in the hands of you and a competent spiritual coach.

● *The "network of friends" resource for emotional health.* People are a major resource in personal support and spiritual growth. The old Beatles song reminds us that we get by "with a little help from our friends." We need others. Leadership is draining work. We give time and energy to others. We help persons in trauma restructure their lives. We work under pressure and against deadlines. Giving to others demands that we receive from others too. Leaders must recharge our batteries in order to lead well.

We need the encouragement of our friends. These intimates help us carry our burdens. They counsel and comfort us while we tackle our problems. The Arab proverb says it well: "You may forget with whom you laughed, but you will never forget with whom you wept."

Whether a formal support or a loosely knit web of friends, our network of friends undergirds our spiritual development. They pray for us and with us. They provide listening ears and shoulders to cry on. They become walking and talking repair kits for refurbishing the frayed edges of our lives. They spare us from isolation and save us from the "Elijah trap" of lonely self-pity (1 Kings 19:10*b*). In all these functions, our network of friends enables us to grow toward God.

● *The "portable seminary" resource for intellectual wholeness.* Options and ideas provide some of the raw materials for spiritual development. "Seedbed" is the literal meaning of the word *seminary.* Actual seminaries are like greenhouses or plant nurseries. These institutions of formal theological education are places where seeds are sprouted before the young plants are transplanted to their permanent garden spots. Seminaries are seedbeds where plants are begun, not a place where full maturity is reached. Spiritual formation is a basic concern of seminaries. But since spirituality is a lifelong process, we must develop ways to continue to grow after we have assumed positions of professional leadership.

Options for spiritual maturing often emerge from idea groups. That is, we join with other ministers whose lives, methods, and styles inspire or instruct us in how we can enhance our spiritual pilgrimages. They model approaches for us, refer us to helpful books and materials, and help us become aware of spiritual growth options. The familiar adage is correct. "Two (or more) heads are better than one."

• *The "mentor in ministry" resource for professional wholeness.* Mentors encourage our vocational and religious development. Those of us who are still young ministers often have mentors. Mentors are older, wiser, and more mature than we are. They teach us, sponsor us, guide us, and become our allies. We respond to them positively because we respect and believe in them. They, in turn, see potential in us and invest energy in cultivating our promise. In many cases, the mentor's dream matches or is even adopted by the apprentice.

Mentors are key resource persons for learning leadership. Since ministry is a vocation learned largely on the job, mentors help us develop professional skills and spiritual depth. Therefore, we are strengthened for today's work and tomorrow's challenges. Mentors contribute to the health and maturity of future generations of leaders.

• *The "temple of God" resource for physical wholeness.* The stewardship of physical health has religious implications. Our bodies are described in the Bible as God's temples (1 Cor. 3:16). Discipline is one link between physical and spiritual health. The link's weakness may be demonstrated in religious leaders in a couple of ways: (1) when exercise enthusiasts have no spiritual discipline or (2) when pious persons are overweight and physically undisciplined.

The physical drain of chairing a tense meeting or preaching an important sermon or counseling an overstressed person is immense. Either we take care of our bodies and our spirits, or we diminish our effectiveness. Rest, good nutrition, recreation and relaxation, and exercise combine to prevent health difficulties.

A regular exercise routine or workout schedule pays dividends in better energy levels now and more vigorous health in the future. Many leaders enjoy athletics because team sports teach the value of cooperation and collaboration more graphically than most other activities.

To sum up, note the spiritual health model below. It looks like a wheel—complete and balanced. Each section supports the other aspects of healthy ministry. If one or two areas are missing or neglected, the wheel may become as useless as a flat tire.

Illustration 25. Ministry Health Model

Overview: Spiritual Disciplines and Leadership

The priorities set by pastoral leaders reflect the place given to spiritual growth. Ideally, our relationship to Christ is and remains consistently the core value of our lives. In order to develop our spiritual lives, a full range of devotional disciplines can be used flexibly and merged with our professional growth. Spiritual maturity is supported by a wholistic and balanced approach to developing our ministries.

Review Questions

1. How can you depict and describe your priorities in ministry?
2. What is the range of devotional disciplines available to pastoral leaders?
3. How do you relate and use the five types of growth resources depicted in the wholistic model?

Notes

1. The model of ministers' priorities and the guidelines for applying the model draw from Ernest E. Mosley's *Priorities in Ministry* (Nashville: Convention Press, 1978), pp. 8-18.
2. Elizabeth O'Connor, *Call to Commitment* (New York: Harper & Row, 1963), p. 94.
3. For a balanced perspective on leadership and spirituality, see William M. Moreman's *Developing Spiritually and Professionally* (Philadelphia: Westminster Press, 1984).
4. Paul Tournier, *To Resist or to Surrender?* (Atlanta: John Knox Press, 1967), p. 57.
5. Moreman, pp. 31-48.
6. These approaches and the model are adapted from my chapter "The Minister of Youth: Developing a System of Support" in Bob R. Taylor, comp., *The Work of the Minister of Youth* (Nashville: Convention Press, 1982), pp. 95-107.

A Selected Bibliography on Spiritual Development and Leadership

Edwards, Tilden. *Spiritual Friend: Reclaiming the Gift of Spiritual Direction.* Ramsey, N.J.: Paulist Press, 1980.

Kelsey, Morton. *The Other Side of Silence.* Ramsey, N.J.: Paulist Press, 1976.

Moreman, William M. *Developing Spiritually and Professionally.* Philadelphia: Westminster Press, 1984.

Mosley, Ernest E. *Priorities in Ministry.* Nashville: Convention Press, 1978.

O'Connor, Elizabeth. *Journey Inward, Journey Outward.* New York: Harper & Row, 1968.

Underhill, Evelyn. *Mysticism.* New York: E. P. Dutton, 1961.

AVOIDING
LEADER BURNOUT

AN ESTIMATED ONE minister in five is burned out. Are ministers more prone to burnout than other persons? Possibly. We ministers may find that our high expectations, when confronted by harsh interpersonal or institutional realities, trigger a loss of will. Burnout, after all, is the ashes of idealism.[1] Ministers pay a steep price when we combine over-responsibility with inflexibility; we become disillusioned dreamers.

When the Fire Dies Out

Idealists who press toward unattainable goals are prime candidates for burnout. These ministers launch into ministry with vigor, optimism, and good intentions. When those of us who are perfectionists persist over a period of time in pursuing our goals without reward, our resources and resiliency are depleted. The wildfire of our early enthusiasm burns out, leaving only the ashes of idealism.

Compare yourself to the prospect list of potential burnouts below. You may find the characteristics form a virtual job description for ministers.

- Energetic crusaders
- Conscientious servants
- Determined goal seekers

- Helpers who play God
- Dynamic, charismatic pacesetters
- Sensitive helpers
- Dreamers who want the best for others
- Purposeful Christians on a clear mission
- Dedicated workaholics

At least three minister types feel the threat of burnout keenly. The "I never get finished" syndrome describes ministers who experience the weight of overload. These helpers know the tyranny of the intangible. We find ministry involves spirituality, growth, and goodness—all intangible and, therefore, difficult to measure.

The "I should be universally liked" syndrome also pressures ministers. Some idealistic young ministers are surprised and disappointed by critics in our congregations. As one recent seminary graduate told me in shocked tones, "I've never had to work with people who didn't like me until now!" This gifted young minister was taking on the impossible responsibility of being universally liked.

The "I hate trivia" syndrome refers to the wide range of expectations—many of them insignificant—ministers are often faced with. Expectations are the high-rent districts of ministry. However, when these expectations revolve around litanies of petty complaints as well as demands for headpatting and handholding, ministers may wish for the opportunity of tackling global concerns. Our motivational reserves are gnawed away by trivial demands.

Who Else Is Smoldering?

Ministers aren't the only professionals who are at risk to burnout. Hospital emergency room workers, coaches, teachers, single parents, law enforcement officers, and air traffic controllers are all under the gun too. In fact, any vocational group made up of persons who work with others, are goal oriented, and take responsibility seriously can (and often do) burn out. These other professionals also understand the burnout dilemma. Consequently, they are usually more alert to the minister's need for a support network than some other church members. Additionally, the sensitive minister will keep a sharp eye peeled toward these pressured members who may need pastoral care when their lives begin to smolder too.

Identifying Lighted Fuses

Burnout seems to follow a fairly predictable sequence of symptoms. Like an ever-tightening whirlpool, burnout begins with vague feelings of fatigue, withdrawal, cynicism, and humorlessness and deepens into more definable indicators.

• "I'm always tired." Persons who are burning out feel chronically weary or even exhausted. These folks wake up to start a new day still feeling tired.
• "I'm not involved in my own life." Burnouts have an "I don't care" attitude. We feel detached from our inner selves, our lives, and our work. Some of us report a sense of standing outside ourselves watching our own emotional erosion.
• "I'm disinterested in my work." Routine and boredom seem to perpetuate themselves. Burnouts feel little or no challenge in our work. We concentrate and listen poorly.
• "I'm irritable." Impatience and quick-temperedness mark the burnout. We are essentially humorless. Our capacity for self-control wanes, and we show the signs of an unusually short fuse.
• "I'm indispensable." Nobody else can do my job as well as I can, burnouts feel. Burnouts paradoxically feel squeezed between a sense of omnipotence and inadequate reserves and resources. We identify with the faithful, but depleted, prophet Elijah after the confrontation on Mt. Carmel: "I, even I only, am left" (1 Kings 19:10b).
• "I work like a beaver, but no one cares." Burnouts think our good work goes unnoticed. Consequently, we feel overworked and under appreciated.

- "Everyone is against me." As burnout deepens, these ministers become more suspicious and may border on displaying hints of paranoia.
- "I'm becoming more forgetful and disoriented." Burnouts have the sensation that thinking requires supreme effort. Remembering names and other facts as well as making logical connections is a labor for burnouts.
- "I'm never completely well." Ailments with psychosomatic dimensions—headaches, colds, sleeplessness, and other nagging health problems—may point to worsening burnout. Chronic illness is often a clue to impending burnout.
- "I'm discouraged about myself and my lot in life." Listlessness, depression, and anger wear us out from the inside. Burnouts invest enormous amounts of energy in protecting our own psyches.
- "I feel nothing." Denial, emotionless, and inner deadness mark the completion of burnout's whirlpool. Nothing really matters. At this stage, burnouts are totally depleted.

Fired Up, Then Burned Out

Burnout can also be examined from a career viewpoint. Four stages have been identified as burnout dampens idealism.[2]

- *Stage One: Enthusiasm.* As a rule, we overvalue the new. Accordingly, we overinvest in new mates, new babies, new cars, as well as new jobs. In ministry we typically attack new tasks with hope and fervor. When intoxicated by our optimism, we set out to bring in the kingdom of God by tomorrow. That's enthusiasm!
- *Stage Two: Stagnation.* The thrills of the workplace are now beginning to dull. Our energies shift from idealism to personal preoccupations with work schedules, money, and time away from the job. Our jobs don't quite measure up to our imaginings. We take less pride in our accomplishments. We are still doing our jobs, but our jobs aren't doing much for us.

• *Stage Three: Frustration.* Apparent powerlessness emerges. We feel that we have little or no control over our life's directions. Work satisfaction is curtailed by too many bureaucratic barriers, too many givens, and too little leverage to change things. Our pessimism is fueled by edginess, fatigue, and irritability. We begin to question our confidence and competence.

• *Stage Four: Apathy.* At this point, our attitude toward work deteriorates into "A job is a job is a job." We are disillusioned but must put bread on the table. Although we must work out of necessity, we shield ourselves by withdrawing emotionally from our ministries. We avoid challenge, do what's absolutely required, go through the motions, and protect ourselves as best we can. We're still at our posts, but we've given up.

There's some good news in this series of stages. Although we may go through the burnout cycle more than once during our ministries, we can learn to recognize and confront burnout creatively.

Am I Burning Out (Or Just Getting Singed)?

Burnout usually happens gradually. Is it possible that you're burning out and haven't recognized it? Let's use an informal checklist to get an indication.

Spotlight the past six months and evaluate your life and work. Using that time frame, rate yourself on a scale from 1 (for "never") to 10 (for "always") on each of the following twenty-six statements. (You should be able to complete this checklist in five minutes or less.)

Mark your first impressions on the inventory below.

1. I'm weary, even when I wake up.

Never	Rarely		Often		Always	
1 2	3 4 5		6 7 8		9 10	

2. I take more medication and drink more caffeine than I used to.

Never	Rarely		Often		Always	
1 2	3 4 5		6 7 8		9 10	

3. I'm short tempered and irritable these days.

Never		Rarely			Often			Always	
1	2	3	4	5	6	7	8	9	10

4. I'm plagued by nagging physical ailments and rarely feel really fit.

Never		Rarely			Often			Always	
1	2	3	4	5	6	7	8	9	10

5. My devotional disciplines are eroding.

Never		Rarely			Often			Always	
1	2	3	4	5	6	7	8	9	10

6. On the job, I feel I'm the only one who really cares about our ministry.

Never		Rarely			Often			Always	
1	2	3	4	5	6	7	8	9	10

7. Relaxing is difficult for me, because I carry my work home with me.

Never		Rarely			Often			Always	
1	2	3	4	5	6	7	8	9	10

8. I need to see what I've accomplished during my work day.

Never		Rarely			Often			Always	
1	2	3	4	5	6	7	8	9	10

9. I demand perfection of myself and others.

Never		Rarely			Often			Always	
1	2	3	4	5	6	7	8	9	10

10. I'm drained from taking care of others all the time.

Never		Rarely			Often			Always	
1	2	3	4	5	6	7	8	9	10

11. I catch myself just going through the motions at work.

Never		Rarely			Often			Always	
1	2	3	4	5	6	7	8	9	10

12. I'm working more and accomplishing less..

Never		Rarely			Often			Always	
1	2	3	4	5	6	7	8	9	10

13. I'm becoming more forgetful.

Never		Rarely			Often			Always	
1	2	3	4	5	6	7	8	9	10

14. I'm becoming less emotionally flexible.

Never		Rarely			Often			Always	
1	2	3	4	5	6	7	8	9	10

15. I dread going to my job.

Never		Rarely			Often			Always	
1	2	3	4	5	6	7	8	9	10

16. I'm becoming more negative and cynical about the people I work with.

Never		Rarely			Often			Always	
1	2	3	4	5	6	7	8	9	10

17. My enjoyment of my work is lessening.

Never		Rarely			Often			Always	
1	2	3	4	5	6	7	8	9	10

18. I feel pressured to compromise my judgment and values.

Never		Rarely			Often			Always	
1	2	3	4	5	6	7	8	9	10

19. I need more feedback on how I do my job.

Never		Rarely			Often			Always	
1	2	3	4	5	6	7	8	9	10

20. My work goes unrecognized and unappreciated.

Never		Rarely			Often			Always	
1	2	3	4	5	6	7	8	9	10

21. I don't laugh much any more, especially at my own shortcomings.

Never		Rarely			Often			Always	
1	2	3	4	5	6	7	8	9	10

22. No one cares how well I do my job.

Never		Rarely			Often			Always	
1	2	3	4	5	6	7	8	9	10

23. I'm powerless to solve the problems and demands my job places on me.

Never		Rarely			Often			Always	
1	2	3	4	5	6	7	8	9	10

24. My job overwhelms the rest of my life.

Never		Rarely			Often			Always	
1	2	3	4	5	6	7	8	9	10

25. No one notices my best work.

Never		Rarely			Often			Always	
1	2	3	4	5	6	7	8	9	10

26. When I review my responses to the twenty-five situations above, I feel my attitude toward my work is worse now than it was six months ago.

Never		Rarely			Often			Always	
1	2	3	4	5	6	7	8	9	10

Illustration 26. Burnout Checklist

Now tally your score on this informal inventory. First, add your numeric responses on the first twenty-five questions. Use this subtotal to help you judge the *magnitude of burnout* in your life and work.

Next, multiply your response on the twenty-sixth question by five. This subtotal reflects the *pace of depletion* you're experiencing.

Finally, add both subtotals. Compare your overall total to the interpretive ranges listed below.

1-100: You aren't even warm yet. Congratulations!

101-200: You're still OK—but monitor yourself for any changes, especially as they relate to the pace of burnout.

201-300: You should act now to take care of yourself. Burnout is a definite possibility—especially at the upper levels of this range.

Dousing the Fire

We can and must confront the burnout process. We can break the cycle of disillusionment. Not just any intervention is productive, however. These false interventions produce temporary results because they only treat symptoms.[3] (1) The "workshop high" effect of some continuing education events fires our idealism again without changing us or our workplace. (2) The "take a day off" remedy may only backlog our work and increase the pressure to catch up later. (3) The "find a new job" intervention is a stopgap at best if we haven't learned from experience and adjusted our attitudes and work habits. Each of these three coping mechanisms can produce a burst of enthusiasm. But since no real changes have been made, the old patterns of depletion are apt to recur in time. The major problem with the strategies mentioned above is that they are remedial measures. They only apply after burnout has occurred.

How can burnout be prevented? By self-care. Although some congregations and ministry agencies provide their ministers with safeguards against the onset of burnout, the primary responsibility for preventing burnout lies with ministers themselves. We can learn to feel and observe the internal signals of burnout in its early stages. Care-givers can and must practice self-care for ourselves through at least four strategies.

Self-care: Managing Our Boundaries

We know that boundaries are dynamic arenas of life. They are more apt to change than other areas. For example, the shoreline where sea and land meet and interact is a boundary that's always in flux. Managing the various personal and professional boundaries of a minister's world is a key element of self-care.

Think of five of these ministerial boundaries. Let's state them as pairs of questions in tension with each other.

● "Who am I as a Christian minister?" in tension with "Who am I as a human being?" This boundary clarifies our calling and identity and reduces our messianic tendencies.
● "Who am I as a private person and family leader?" in tension with "Who am I as a minister and a congregational leader?" This boundary distinguishes between our personal and professional lives.
● "Who am I as an individual?" in tension with "Who are the persons I minister to?" This boundary defines us as separate from the persons we minister to and allows us to say "yes" and "no" more clearly to ministry demands.
● "What are my vocational obligations? " in tension with "What are my avocational opportunities?" This boundary separates work from play and cuts down on workaholism.
● "What am I able to do and not able to do?" in tension with "What do people expect of me?" This boundary aids in separating realistic from unrealistic expectations as well as legitimate needs from superhuman demands or from trivia.

Boundary management is a preventive measure against burnout. Boundary questions aren't easy to answer, however. In fact, they are never finally answered. These ongoing issues remind us how dynamic the boundary areas of our lives and work are. Boundaries also pinpoint the high risk issues for potential burnout.

Self-care: Monitoring Our Resources

Monitoring patterns of spiritual depletion and psychosomatic ailments provides us with another avenue of preventive self-care. Tracking our feelings of fatigue and potential burnout may be as simple as making, analyzing, and acting on two listings.

First, make a "drain list" of the situations, activities, and relationships that drain you physically, emotionally, and spiritually. This ledger sheet gives you a listing of your "expenditures" in living and working. Next, make a "recharge list" of the situations, activities, and relationships that renew you. This list reminds you of your "income" sources.

Now, take each list and rank order the items from the most intense drains and recharges to the least intense. This step will clarify which drains and recharges are most critical and which are marginal. Examine your ranking of the "drain list" and ask yourself some questions. Can I lop off some of the lower ranking items? Can I delegate some of the middle range items? Can I cope more effectively with some of the top level items? Turn now to your "recharge list" and question it closely. How vital are the lower ranking items to me now? Should I concentrate on strengthening the middle range items? Can I recommit myself to the highest ranking items?

Monitoring our lives helps us keep tabs on where we are in our lives and work. Planning can be done and preventive steps can be taken from the information we gain from monitoring activities.

Self-care: Replenishing Our Reserves

No minister can give, give, and give without receiving too. If we don't replenish ourselves, we may be tempted to give out and give up. Ministers need the support of encouraging relationships and accessible resources for replenishment.

Visualize our support networks as cubes. Each of the six sides symbolizes a major source of support for ministry. (1) Spiritual relationships and resources form the front face of our support cube. Our relationship to God and our devotional disciplines are the central facet of this asset for ministry. (2) Our families and spouses provide the support from the back face of the cube. These encouragers literally provide us backing amid the varied demands of ministry. (3) Denominational leaders and resources make up the top face of the cube. These supportive assets funnel all kinds of helpful materials to us. (4) Congregational and institutional resources comprise the bottom or undergirding face of the cube. (5) Our cluster of peers provides the right side face of the cube. (6) Other community helping professionals form the left side face of the cube. Look at the support cube as an integrated whole. If any face of the cube is shaky or missing, the overall network is weakened and creates special vulnerability to burnout.

Self-care: Safety Valve Strategies for Us

Occasionally we discover we're in the midst of burnout, and remedial steps are our only options. Then emergency measures afforded by safety valve strategies are necessary. Frequently, the best safety valves are persons who believe in us enough that they will level with us.

When burnout has occurred, supportive relationships are apparently the only reliable cure. Burnouts need listeners, problem solvers, feedback givers, and patient friends who offer (but don't force) help. Counseling and career assessment are also useful approaches in confronting habitual cycles of burnout.

Bulletin! Lay Leaders Burn Out Too!

Lay ministers are plagued by burnout too. Some congregations are discovering basic ways to confront this challenge.

● Help members identify their spiritual gifts and minister out of those gifts. Staying power resides in our strengths.
● Keep the congregation's dream before the membership. People gain encouragement from the conviction that their ministry efforts are focused on the heart of their congregation's mission.
● Use participative decision-making approaches. Imple-

mentation is more likely to be ensured when the congregation's policy makers are also its ministry activists.

• Nurture spiritual growth. To try to do God's work without a sense of God's power is a sure route to burnout.

• Train your workers. Confident persons are more effective and less frustrated.

• Reward good ministry. Recognizing volunteers for productive service builds up the morale level of the entire congregation.

Overview: Avoiding Leader Burnout

Burnout is a threat to idealists. However, the signals of impending burnout and the stages of burnout can be recognized and confronted. Self-care provides the key preventive approach for ministers—clergy and lay—who act to keep burnout at arm's length.

Review Questions

1. Who are the prime candidates for burnout?
2. What are the stages of the burnout cycle?
3. How do you interpret your score on the burnout inventory?
4. What are the basic self-care strategies?

Notes

1. The perspectives in this chapter are largely adapted from my article, "Burnout, the Ashes of Idealism," from *Search*, Summer 1982: © Copyright 1982 by the Sunday School Board of the Southern Baptist Convention. All rights reserved. Used by permission.
2. Jerry Edelwich, *Burn-Out: Stages of Disillusionment in the Helping Professions* (New York: Human Sciences Press, 1980).
3. Herbert J. Freudenberger, *Burn-Out: The High Cost of High Achievement* (Garden City, N.Y.: Doubleday & Co., 1980), pp. 85-121.

A Selected Bibliography on Leader Burnout

Bellak, Leopold. *Overload: The New Human Condition.* New York: Human Sciences Press, 1975.

Edelwich, Jerry. *Burn-Out: Stages of Disillusionment in the Helping Professions.* New York: Human Sciences Press, 1980.

Faulkner, Brooks R. *Burnout in Ministry.* Nashville: Broadman Press, 1981.

Freudenberger, Herbert J. *Burn-Out: The High Cost of High Achievement.* Garden City, N.Y.: Doubleday & Co., Anchor Books, 1980.

Rassieur, Charles L. *Stress Management for Ministers.* Philadelphia: Westminster Press. 1982.

Veninga, Robert L., and Spradley, James P. *The Work/Stress Connection: How to Cope with Job Burnout.* Boston: Little, Brown & Co., 1981.

— 17 —

FAMILY
LEADERSHIP

LEADERS IN MINISTRY are expected to be family leaders too. The relationship between the congregation and the minister's family calls for balance. However, personal and professional balance can be upset in at least two ways. (1) Ministry leaders may neglect their families and, by biblical standards, render themselves unworthy of congregational leadership. The Bible clearly states that pastors are disqualified from congregational leadership if they don't lead their families toward health and stability (1 Tim. 3:4-5). Additionally, church leaders who don't care for their families are considered to have disowned the faith (1 Tim. 5:8). (2) Ministers may overinvest in the congregation and commit corporate bigamy by "marrying" both job and family. When priorities are tilted toward the church too exclusively, ministers and their families suffer. Clergy families' suffering may take the form of neglect more than betrayal.

Danger: Marital Dry Rot

Ministers don't divorce as frequently as the general population. Neither do ministers' children characteristically go to the dogs. In fact, ministers' children become leaders in a higher proportion than do other youngsters. Then, all's well in the minister's household? Not necessarily. The pressures that occur in other marriages, especially the problems unique to professional persons, apply to ministers too. But there's one special hazard that ministers cope with regularly.

Marriage counselor Wallace Denton uses the metaphor of "dry rot" to describe what happens when busy people take their marriages for granted. Denton's dry rot image is drawn from gardening. A contrast between white potatoes and sweet potatoes provides Denton's danger signal.

Compare how these kinds of vegetables deteriorate. White potatoes decay dramatically. They stink, calling everyone's attention to their rotting state. Sweet potatoes, on the other hand, rot by silently dehydrating without any smell. These sweet potatoes wither away and become a dried up skin without any flesh inside. Marriages decay similarly. Some go bad dramatically and call attention to themselves. Others simply erode, dry up, and lose their vitality. That erosion is best described as dry rot and is the more likely possibility for ministers' marriages.[1]

Pressures in the Parsonage

Ministers' homes experience the same general pressures as other professionals' households—but they are even more visible in the community. Several pressure points plague ministers' families, according to their own reports.

• The "never at home" pressure. Time management is consistently the most troublesome issue ministers and our families report.
• The "church above all" pressure. Congregational bigamy, being "married" to a spouse and a job at same time, is the home front result of worshiping our work.
• The "equal love for all" pressure. Ministers obviously can't play favorites and create teacher's (or preacher's) pets within the congregation. But when congregational relationships and resources are deliberately bypassed by the minister's family in the name of equality, our local support network is usually weakened.

- The "glass house" pressure. Ministers' families often sense that we are on display. As one pastor's wife observed, "I feel like a guppy in a lighted aquarium!"
- The "model family" pressures. Flaws, faults, and foibles in the minister's household are often held up to the mirror of congregational and community evaluation.
- The "drive in" pressure. Some ministers' homes—especially parsonages, and more especially those parsonages located next door to the church—are considered open to church members, thus reducing the privacy of the minister's family to a minimum.
- The "moving van" pressure. Mobility is a negative issue in many denominations. Ministers tend to uproot our families with regularity.
- The "shrinking dollar" problem. Ministry usually provides a modest income. The expectations of the congregation and the assault of inflation keep some pressure on the ordinary minister's family budget.

Leading—Stage by Stage

Marriages and families move through stages and phases. As marriages mature and change, families grow and age. Stage by stage, our home leadership needs and circumstances ripen throughout our life cycle. In fact, when viewed across the span of our lives, we experience several marriages within our marriage and several families within our family.[2] Healthy homes strengthen and grow as time passes just as naturally as shedding baby teeth makes room for permanent ones.

Let's examine eight marriage and family stages and the leadership needs appropriate for each stage. Typically, we're more concerned about the stage we're currently in than the others. But keep two facts in mind: (1) each of us is likely to experience all of these stages ourselves sooner or later, and (2) the varied marriages and families we minister to demand that we have a knowledge of and appreciation for all the different stages.

Stage One: Our "Happily Ever After" Homes

"Happily ever after"—newlyweds believe that fairy-tale ending. The early months of a new marriage often abound with romantic fantasies. Life is viewed simply—we love each other—and romantically—our lives are endless rainbows, roses, and rendevous. We will live happily ever after.

But relationships are two-sided. So the "I never knew's" soon set in. I never knew you'd wake up cranky every morning. I never knew you couldn't balance a checkbook. I never knew you hated to put out the garbage too. The "I never knew's" quickly offset the "happily ever after's." Romance has collided with reality; the honeymoon is over.

Much of the first two or three years of marriage is spent discovering and adjusting to the two-sidedness of husband-wife relationships. Growing closer and staying separate. Finding similarities and being surprised by differences. Loving most of the time and disliking occasionally. Fighting and making up. The process of mutual discovery may be sometimes painful. On the other hand, this growth process is necessary if we are to see our mates as whole persons, not as one-dimensional mannekins.

The "happily ever after" homes provide several leadership opportunities:

● Establishing a new home unit with an identity separate from our families of origin.
● Negotiating healthy, satisfying, and comfortable marriage relationships and roles.
● Learning to disagree agreeably.
● Viewing our individual differences as features of personality, not as faults or flaws.

Stage Two: Our "Making Ends Meet" Homes

The dual career household is now more a way of life than a stage. Many families need two paychecks to make the ends of their budget meet in the middle. Some husbands and wives didn't plan for their life styles to require two incomes, but the American economy and inflation forced them to adopt their "Plan B"—dual careers. A few of these households figure they will pursue two incomes only temporarily—until a house is paid for or children's educations are provided for.

Dual career marriages and households take on an ungainly quality, a bifocal character. Managing the mix of careers, family roles, and household responsibilities is a difficult balancing act. Keeping this amalgam working and growing requires commitment and flexibility.

The "making ends meet" family calls for leadership at several crucial points:

• Keeping careers from becoming a wedge between husband and wife or parent and child.
• Guarding against making jobs the primary at-home conversation topic.
• Developing a household partnership with shared roles and responsibilities.
• Molding a joint career relationship with understandings about time, money, and work-home balance.

Stage Three: Our "Bundle of Joy" Homes

Parenthood creates family in the traditionally fullest sense of the word. The birth of children is referred to as "a blessed event" or a "bundle of joy." Children's births afford an occasion to reaffirm the love of parents for each other and their mutual future.

Two trends are changing the "bundle of joy" home. (1) Americans are waiting until later in life to have children. The over thirty age group is the only American age cluster with an increasing childbearing rate. (2) Child-free marriages are becoming more common. This option is a matter of choice rather than a medical complication.

The introduction of new babies into households inaugurates a range of new strains on the family network. Parents feel a loss of personal freedom; no longer can they change their schedules at a whim. Sometimes babies are experienced as rivals or replacements. The husband-wife relationship, especially its sexual dimension, is altered to some extent. The parents of our families of origin become grandparents and view our families differently now. Child care becomes a major responsibility. The child-rearing behaviors of our families of origin frequently are mirrored clearly in our households now that we have children of our own.

Parenting is considered the most stressful and dangerous process married folks engage in, according to some counselors. On the average, American marriages that end in divorce last slightly more than six years and involve one child. When husbands and wives can't healthily incorporate a baby into family circles, the marriage is under siege.

Childbearing places a variety of leadership demands on families:

• Keeping the core of family living—the husband-wife relationship—enriched.
• Seeing children as unique persons in the family cluster.
• Recognizing children as dependent beings who need the love and care of two parents.
• Developing a personalized parenting style.
• Guarding against becoming so absorbed in parenting that spouses neglect each other.

Stage Four: Our "Expanding World" Homes

Childrearing usually matches our adult life stage transition from our twenties into our thirties. At that time in our lives we decide to "get serious" and "make a contribution." Rearing our children is an aspect of approaching life more soberly and productively. One tension in "expanding world" homes is the conflict between childrearing and career advance.

When children enter school, their worlds expand radically. They begin to experience a life apart from home. Their social and intellectual horizons explode. New friends, independent schedules, and the importance of an influencing person from beyond the family—a teacher—stretch youngsters' perspectives and cause them to investigate life beyond home and hearth.

For some parents, launching children into the world stirs feelings of loss and rivalry. To illustrate, a minister friend of mine reported that he stood at his living room window on his daughter's first day of school and watched the big, yellow school bus "swallow her up." He was experiencing the separation anxieties typical of an "expanding world" home. Childrearing opens the door to self-knowledge for parents as well as for the children.

Effective leadership is vital to homes at the childrearing stage of the "expanding world":

● Resisting over-investing emotionally in child-centeredness to the detriment of the home's core, the husband-wife relationship.
● Dealing with the power struggles over children's friends, family scheduling, and budgeting.
● Coping with deadening routines that squeeze the zest out of relationships and open the door to the seven-year itch.

Stage Five: Our "Breaking Away" Homes

Parent-teen relationships are potentially fraught with tension. Teens storm the family fortress in an attempt to carve out their own identities; parents defend the ramparts in order to maintain some semblance of stability and control. "Breaking away" describes the process of facing the tempting thrills of the forbidden. The inevitable antagonism between generations is obvious at this stage.

In a way, "breaking away" homes are caught in the crossfires between teens' adolescence and parents' middlescence. The teen years revolve around the search for the answers to two questions: Who am I? and What will I do with my life? Midlife revolves around the same two issues. Since both generations are struggling with the same problems at two distinctly different stages of life, the possibility of double binds occurring in the family is likely.

Parenting teens is a challenge. Teens want more freedom; parents need to turn loose wisely. Teens need wings; parents provide roots. Teens are becoming young adults; full-time parenting is drawing to a close. The challenge of parent-child relationships is in talking, listening, and negotiating so that all parties win.

Husbands and wives experience both richness and routine at midlife. The changing tides of marriage bring companionship and devotion as well as the risks of taking each other for granted. Midlife marriages invite recommitment as well as the enticements of moving off in separate directions. An increasing threat to clergy marriages at this life stage is dry rot, the eroding of untended relationships.

The "breaking away" homes demand steady leadership:

• Realizing some tension and anger are natural when family limits are tested.

• Shifting disciplinary styles to include teenagers in family rule setting pocesses.

• Creating flexible family boundaries that blend freedom and protection.

• Resisting the temptation to become a pal to our teens in an attempt to relive our adolescence vicariously.

• Renewing the husband-wife relationship and learning to live together again as a couple in an emptying household.

Stage Six: Our "Untying the Apron Strings" Homes

Sending our children out into the world on their own is an exciting and frightening life stage. On the excitement side of the ledger, at this stage older children discover each other as friends of and mentors to younger siblings. On the frightening side of the ledger, the family shrinks. This shrinkage is particularly threatening in two circumstances: (1) when the family has become child-centered and the husband-wife relationship has atrophied, and (2) when the wife and mother has adopted such a traditionalized role that the exit of children from her home means the loss of her identity and reason for being.

Loosening our parenting links to our children can trigger obsolescence anxiety. We feel life's deadlines beginning to crowd in on us. We want to leave a legacy; our children are one important part of what we will leave behind when we're gone. In a symbolic sense, the independent pilgrimages of our launched children allow us to extend our influence beyond the untied apron strings.

Leadership issues crop up at this life stage also:

• Granting adult status to our children in the younger generation and passing the torch to them.
• Deciding what kind of personal and family legacies we will leave.
• Dealing with changes, losses, and aging.
• Easing the breakaway guilt of some children.

Stage Seven: Our "Empty Nest" Homes

Now the children are gone from home. Spouses look at each other across the meal table without the buffers and distractions of children. The vitality of the husband-wife relationship is more noticeable during the "empty nest" stage than probably ever before or after.

The "empty nest" era can be especially traumatic for some couples who had children early. We may find our home nest emptying at the same time we are experiencing our individual midlife crises. As smaller families become a more common pattern, this multiple crisis possibility looms larger.

The "empty nest" home is a mixture of good news and bad news. Grandparenthood, for example, is a pleasant "empty nest" process for most of us. The parenting function between grandparents and grandchildren is generally more relaxed. The bad news of the "empty nest" stage involves the emotional and physical adjustments we face naturally at late midlife. Women face menopause (and men metapause). Tragically, we see our friends confront health crises, divorces, and even death.

A mixed experience is receiving an adult child back into our home after career crises or marital problems. These happenings offer opportunities to love and understand them but may also create mutual pressures, expenses, and guilt.

Like an empty shell found on the beach, the empty nest reminds us that the original inhabitants have moved on. Some discomfort about what to do with our lives now is offset by the available solitude to find our centers of gravity again. Best of all, both spouses can grow together and individually.

Numerous leader challenges face persons at the "empty nest" stage:

• Refocusing on our marriage rather than on our larger family circle.
• Becoming in-laws and accepting sons-in-law and daughters-in-law into our family network.
• Nurturing a new generation as grandparents.
• Preparing for retirement.
• Assisting dependent parents and learning how interdependent generations relate.

Stage Eight: Our "Three Generation" Homes

Life's summing up stages combine three generations—grandparents, parents, and children. But for many families, the third generation involves only grandmother. American widows outnumber widowers by a ratio of three to one. On the average, American women outlive men by nine years. Widowhood introduces an unfamiliar life style for many traditional widows; they are forced to put themselves first rather than their families.

Some third generation persons experience great-grandparenthood, an even rarer role. These elder members of the family system represent continuity and function as family historians. They can help younger generations appreciate their family roots. On the other hand, failing health and fixed incomes may cause them to rely on the younger generations they have shaped.

Three generations relating to one another create unique leadership needs:

- Giving the freedom and power to our children and grandchildren to be self-directing.
- Affirming the past and the present as well as living creatively in the present and future with most of life already past.
- Enjoying natural alliances with grandchildren.

How to Strengthen Minister-Family Relationships

Seasoned ministers have found a range of actions that ensure better relationships in their families.[3] Consider these possibilities.

- Set family goals. As a family group, negotiate our family's needs for communication, openness, encouragement, rules and discipline, and time together.[4]
- Enlist the congregation's help in clarifying work expectations. After limits are set, ask the congregation's support in protecting time agreements.
- Schedule time together as a family, as a couple, and as parent-child pairs or groups and commit to protect that time.
- Take advantage of denominational and ecumenical resources to participate in family enrichment and in marriage enrichment.
- Participate in self-discovery experiences, such as growth groups or counseling, in order to ensure that personal needs for recognition, power, or achievement aren't pursued at the expense of either our family or our congregation.
- Work together as a spouse and/or family team in ministry. While this approach is impractical for many clergy families, some persons, especially women, have apparently chosen to marry ministers because they weren't comfortable with being ordained themselves.[5]

Overview: Family Leadership

Ministers' families provide a leadership opportunity. Dry rot, pressures common to ministers' households, and the challenges of various stages of family living call for assertive family leaders. In the face of a variety of strains, ministers and our families have discovered creative actions to keep our homes healthy and wholesome.

Review Questions

1. What is dry rot in ministers' marriages?
2. What are some of the pressures that plague ministers' homes?
3. What are the leadership challenges families face at each life stage?

Notes

1. Wallace Denton, "Family Conflicts of the Modern Minister," *Baptist Program*, March 1974, p. 8.
2. This material on family stages is largely adapted from Robert D. and Carrie L. Dale, *Marriage: Partnership of the Committed* (Nashville: Sunday School Board of the Southern Baptist Convention, 1983) and from Robert D. Dale, "The Bible Speaks to Changing Family Stages" in W. Douglas Cole, ed., *Strengthening the Family* (Cary, N.C.: Baptist State Convention of North Carolina, 1984), pp. 52-61.
3. Charles H. Ellzey and Paul M. Dietterich, "Strengthening Clergy-Family Relationships," *The Center Letter*, August 1972, pp. 1-2.
4. Lyndon E. Whybrew, *Minister, Wife and Church: Unlocking the Triangles* (Washington, D.C.: Alban Institute, 1984).
5. "Occupation: Preacher's Wife," *Human Behavior*, July 1976, p. 38.

A Selected Bibliography on Family Leadership

Bailey, Robert W., and Bailey, Mary Frances. *Coping with Stress in the Minister's Home.* Nashville: Broadman Press, 1979.

Douglas, William. *Ministers' Wives.* New York: Harper & Row, 1965.

Hunt, Richard A. *Ministry and Marriage.* Dallas: Ministry Studies Board, 1976.

Lavender, Lucille. *They Cry, Too!* New York: Hawthorn Books, 1976.

Mace, David and Vera. *What's Happening to Clergy Marriages?* Nashville: Abingdon Press, 1980.

Nyberg, Kathleen Neill. *The Care and Feeding of Ministers: From the Wife's Point of View.* Nashville: Abingdon Press, 1961.

Whybrew, Lyndon E. *Minister, Wife and Church: Unlocking the Triangles.* Washington, D.C.: Alban Institute, 1984.

— 18 —

CAREER
DEVELOPMENT
FOR LEADERS

DECISIONS PROVIDE US with levers to take charge of our careers in ministry. Deciding whom to count on for vocational encouragement, recognizing our professional anchors, preparing for varied stages in our lives and careers, and planning for career assessment and development are each concrete actions leaders can take to enrich our vocational lives. Choose, cultivate, act now, and grow in professional competence.

Guides for the Vocational Journey

None of us lives in complete isolation. Christians belong to a family of faith. These encouragers provide us with a "cloud of witnesses" (Heb. 12:1); they help us find our niche in Christian service and chart our progress on our career pilgrimage. At least three types of persons are pivotal guides for us on our vocational journey: mentors, models, and our inner circle of friends.

Mentors: Guides for Where We Want to Go

Mentor, in Greek legend a friend and adviser of Odysseus and a guardian to Odysseus' son, played the role of motivator and helper in attaining goals. Mentors provide similar guidance for us too. Generally speaking, mentors are a generation or so older than their apprentices, are already active in the work world the apprentice aspires to, and help us move into the responsibility of professional-level service. Mentors are sponsors, advisers, teachers, and counselors for us.

The mentor-apprentice relationship is an intense and unusual one. Mentors are part friend, part parent, but fully neither. Mentor relationships are ordinarily short-term—from two to ten years—and tend to end somewhat painfully. The end result of mentorship is that we are aided in fulfilling our vocational dream.

Ask yourself these questions about your mentors. Who are (or have been) my mentors? How have they helped me personally and professionally? Have I recognized their contributions to my career and thanked them for mentoring me?

Models: Guides for What We Want to Become

Models help us (1) identify the type of person we want to become and (2) see some qualities to mirror and develop. Goals are easier to set and pursue when we can visualize others who have reached the same or similar goals. By the same token, changes are easier to make when we can imitate others whom we admire.

Note an important distinction. Mentors are persons we know well and have seen work; models aren't necessarily close acquaintances. Models may be historical figures, childhood heroes, program personalities or special lecturers, teachers, or media persons. Whether alive or dead, these special guides provide us role models of whom to become or how to work.

Pose these inquiries to yourself about your models. Who are they? Why have they been (or were they) chosen? What characteristics or behaviors of theirs have I modeled on? Have I thanked them for their contributions to my professional growth?

Inner Circle: Guides Who Encourage Us to Grow

Leaders tend to develop a cluster of friends and confidants. Jesus had an inner circle of friends—Peter,

James, and John. Relationships of this high quality reflect those special persons who believe in us, encourage us, forgive us, give us the benefit of the doubt, pray for us, and trust us. An inner circle might include our spouse, best friend, kin, and professional peers. These folks support and guide us daily as we move through our careers. Except for unusual cases, inner circles of encouragers tend to be fairly small.

Explore your support network of encouragers. List them first. Then, evaluate the strength and breadth of your inner circle carefully. Use these "filters" to test your support network. (1) Strike all the names of family members from your list. Don't misunderstand. Typically, our family members are our most reliable encouragers. However, we need more persons than our spouses and children as confidants, or we will tend to overload and strain these crucial relationships. Furthermore, these loved ones are biased in our favor and aren't always able to provide us with reliable feedback. (2) Of the remaining names, strike through the names of supportive persons who live more than one hundred miles from us or with whom we don't have direct contact at least every six weeks. Genuine encouragement demands accessibility. (3) If names remain on your list, strike off any names of persons who work at the same vocation as you or who are in the same denominational family as you. Support systems sometimes deteriorate into shop talk rather than dealing with the deeper, more crucial issues. Don't miss the opportunity to show your appreciation for the members of your inner circles.

Others are important to us. They help us discover our career directions. They empower us to pursue our vocation. Mentors, models, and inner circles need to be cultivated and nurtured. Don't hesitate to reach out to your special people for guidance. And, especially, don't forget to say thanks for their guidance and stabilizing influence.

Anchoring Your Career

Career anchors are provided by the clusters of abilities, values, and needs you've discovered in yourself as well as the sense of selfhood you've achieved. Taken together, these factors energize, integrate, and stabilize you vocationally throughout your career. In business and industry, managers find competence, security, autonomy, and creativity to be important anchors.[1]

Several other categories of career anchors may relate to the ministry and other helping professions:

• *Calling*—Ministers generally have a strong sense of calling. We either claim a special leading ("God directed me to become a minister") or a natural leading ("I responded to others' needs and decided ministry was something I could do well"). An experience of calling lends an anchor to our careers.[2] For many ministers this sense of calling undergirds all other anchors mentioned below.

• *Identity*—Work can define us. We may find our basic self-definition in titles, symbols, clerical dress, or other external factors. For example, some ministers insist on "Reverend" or "Pastor" as a mode of address and, more importantly, as our identity.

• *Service*—Most of us in ministry have been taught to think of others and show concern for them before ourselves. Helping others can become an important end in itself for those of us in ministry.

• *Influence*—Many people listen to ministers. They ask us informational questions, seek our advice about decisions, and lean on us for support in crises. We gain some power over them; we can control their lives to some extent.

• *Variety*—The ministry is a generalist role. We're called on to become jacks-of-all-trades. The sheer range of challenges ministers face allows us to (or demands that we) develop and express a vast array of talents and interests.

• *Skill*—Experience in ministry, theological training, and continuing education helps ministers gain competence. Feeling skilled and comfortable in proclamation, caring, and leadership situations (see chapter 1) increases our confidence in our ability to minister effectively.

Did you find your own career anchors in one or several of these already mentioned above? These factors give you emotional and spiritual stability zones for career evaluation and development.

Leadership and Career Stages

Our lives move through a series of stages. Each stage is important. Each phase has built-in challenges and decisions. If we make responsible decisions about the stage we're in, we're better prepared to handle the next stage's opportunities. Since careers are personal expressions of our sense of Christian calling, we must take charge of our vocational choices and career planning.

Each stage has its own texture and character. Some stages are stable and structured; others are full of instability, shakiness, and discomfort. In pendulum fashion, our lives move back and forth between relatively stable periods and unstructured phases. Four fairly predictable career stages are spotlighted here with some of their applications to ministry noted.[3]

Novice Adults and Career Leadership

Novice adults span the years from late teens to nearly thirty. These young adults enjoy some suspension of expectations while they are in the educational process or are learning their craft and are still considered young. Novices are allowed to take less responsibility and are given more latitude to make mistakes.

Novice adults concentrate on five issues. (1) Novices define dreams. They envision their life-style and career goals. This imagined possibility generates vitality and motivation. (2) Novices enlist mentors. Their mentors act as guides and sponsors. Mentors usually are one or two generations older than the novice and occupy a rung on the career ladder the novice aspires to. Mentors see potential and invest coaching effort in the novice. Consequently, mentor-novice relationships tend to be intense. In ministry, mentor relationships often follow a "son in the ministry" pattern, as with Paul and Timothy. Females in ministry, therefore, typically find mentorships somewhat more difficult to develop than male ministers.

(3) Novices focus on the work world. The first professional job is crucial and often has a life-shaping impact on novices. That is, outlook on ministry is heavily influenced by early ministry experiences. (4) Novices choose mates. Additionally, some novices meet a special, opposite-sexed encourager who believes in the novice fully. (5) Novices learn to build enduring relationships. We learn how to love others responsibly.

A range of actions is appropriate for novices in shaping careers:

• Model career dreams on Jesus' vision of the kingdom of God.
• Allow your sense of calling to deepen but don't rush the process by making a final choice prematurely. Studies indicate that many leaders are in their early thirties before they commit themselves to the vocation they eventually make a long-term contribution to. Jesus, Paul, Luther, and Wesley are notable examples.
• Accept the guidance of mature mentors. Ministry is an on-the-job-training vocation. Apprentice relationships are valuable for novices.
• Experiment with approaches and methods in order to develop a comfortable ministry style as early in your careers as possible.
• Cultivate the friendships you make in school and early ministry. These relationships will be important links in your support systems for the rest of your ministry.

Junior Adults and Career Leadership

Junior adults in the age range from the late twenties until the early thirties get serious about life. They stand up to life and settle into heavier responsibilities. Junior adults are in between, no longer novices but not yet senior adults.

Junior adults are characterized by several interests. (1) They put down roots. At the beginning of the adult stage, juniors examine their life structures and usually decide they want "more." They take on more family accountability and are somewhat more likely to feel marital stress. (2) Junior adults invest lots of energy in career advancement. They move on toward their dream and work on their craft. (3) Juniors become more aware of emotional and spiritual needs. With the early signals of aging beginning to show up, junior adults feel an internal push to find better questions rather than relying on all-purpose answers. (4) Junior adults become more independent. In the words of Paul, they have grown up and, as a result, "gave up childish ways" (1 Cor. 13:11).

Influencing behaviors are open to junior adults who plan to become more intentional in career development:

• Develop a support network. The giving of ministry must be balanced by receiving. Even Jesus called the Twelve, in part, "to be with him" (Mark 3:14).
• Keep marriage and family relationships renewed. These relationships are crucial. They shouldn't be taken for granted. No relationship grows on autopilot.
• Plan for continuing education. A study time and a reading program are basic. Seminars, workshops, and professional skill development opportunities should be strategically selected to enhance talents and offset limitations.[4]
• Cultivate devotional disciplines. Use a variety of creative approaches to avoid staleness or routine.
• Guard physical and mental health. Exercise, eat healthily and regularly, and manage stress levels carefully.
• Establish family financial planning practices early in ministry. Set aside money for retirement, childrens' educations, and special professional and family projects.

• Don't get too impatient about career advance. Remember that Jesus and Paul began their ministries as mature persons. Like many junior adults, they apparently discovered that they were old enough to have a ministry dream and still young enough to implement their vision.

Midlife Adults and Career Leadership

Midlife adults, roughly from age thirty-five and forty-five, frequently experience a "midlife crisis." The discomfort of midlife for some of us is the realization that some persons now see us as old. Aging is rarely fun, especially in youth-worshiping America. From a career viewpoint, crisis causes us to stop for a major life evaluation.

A range of career issues faces adults at midlife. (1) Life structures are examined and dreams are revised. Midlife and midcareer find many ministers feeling plateaued and stuck. Some fear having succeeded too easily and peaked too soon. Others feel they have failed or gotten derailed from the career ladder. Most grapple with middlescence, a renewal of identity and career definitions. For males, our late thirties and early forties are traditionally the years of deepest re-evaluation. We may feel panic, wondering if life's prime opportunities have already passed us by.

(2) Midlife adults feel threatened by obsolescence. The years between our middle thirties and middle forties are filled with deadlines. We ask ourselves, "If not now, when?" We pare down our interests and put all our eggs into one basket. Like Paul at midlife, we narrow the focus of life and commit ourselves to this "one thing I do" (Phil. 3:13). (3) Midlife adults create legacies. Symbolically, we live on through our children and through the results of ministry programs, building projects, and our words both spoken and written. (4) The home nest empties for midlifers. This is often the era of the returning father, when we shift our life direction somewhat away from career and more toward home. Additionally, men frequently sense a softer aspect of our personalities emerging. (5) Midlife adults experience more nagging health difficulties.

Career leadership can be expressed at this stage through a variety of actions (Some of the steps listed below are applicable to other stages also.)

• Cultivate a support network.
• Invest in marriage and family enrichment.
• Research midlife issues. So much has been written in popular and technical sources about middle age that information on this stage is readily available.
• Consider career assessment with a vocational guidance consultant.
• Stay fresh devotionally.
• Get regular exercise.
• Become a mentor. After forty, we are more apt to provide mentorship than to need it.
• Clarify ministry priorities. With less available time and energy left, a sharply defined life goal is even more important in ministry stewardship.
• Become a lifelong learner. Consider a Doctor of Ministry program or some other structured study option to update information and upgrade skill levels.
• Celebrate spiritual gifts and personal contributions to others through ministry. Midlifers have a ministry record to evaluate; rejoice in the growth in yourself and in others whose lives you've touched.

Senior Adults and Career Leadership

Senior adults, generally persons in the age range of the fifties and sixties, look for purpose and meaning in life and work. Seniors discover that most Americans think anyone past fifty is old. Soon they will join America's largest minority—retirees. Aging will come with either comfort and satisfaction or bitterness, anger, and disgust.

Senior adults face a range of life and career situations. (1) Senior adults transfer hope to the next generation. As Elijah passed his mantle on to Elisha, older adults pass a legacy of leadership on to new generations. (2) Senior adults experience lessening energy. Many congregations prefer energy over experience and overlook the mature leadership senior adults can provide. Some seniors also live with an erosion of health. As a Virginia pastor observed when he retired at sixty-one after having had a heart attack at fifty-nine, "You get worn out in this kind of work." (3) Senior adults accept "followship." Many take on an important elder statesman role.

Senior adults have a number of career leadership options open.

• Prepare for retirement. Plan for both the emotional and financial adjustments. Use vacations as indicators of how the transition to retirement will go; vacations break into our routines and test our flexibility.
• Continue to learn. Senior adults adjust learning style by using ears more than eyes and by writing ideas down rather than trying to remember so many things.
• Stay physically active. Walking is an excellent exercise for senior adults.
• Take the risks of new ministry. Maturity affords perspectives and abilities that enhance launching out into a fresh challenge.
• Work smarter, not harder. Senior adults can apply the lessons of maturity to professional tasks and can teach others some legitimate shortcuts.
• Learn to distinguish between self-concern and self-absorption. Seniors must be good stewards of health and opportunities. They don't, however, necessarily have to become so self-absorbed as to bore friends by talking only about themselves and the distant past.
• Remember that ministry is an attitude as well as a role. When we retire, we lose the role of minister in a congregation or agency. But if we maintain a helpful attitude and reasonable accessibility, we will find our ministry welcomed by some others. Caleb took on his toughest ministry challenges at age eighty-five (Josh. 14:6-14).

Life Transitions and Career Crises

The pendulum swing from one life stage to another creates the occasion for career crises to emerge. Three crises apply particularly to ministers. Each of these crises opens the door for career adjustments or even career change. (1) The first predictable crisis in ministry revolves around our first full-time ministry post. As novices, our initial experiences in ministry shape our perspectives toward our work and influence our sense of professional competency. (2) The second evaluation point typically occurs about five years into our careers in ministry. This crisis coincides roughly with the transition from the novice to the junior adult stage and pressures us to contribute something to our professional world. (3) The third crossroad happens during midlife and often raises the issue of obsolescence.

Each of these crises provides the opportunity for taking charge of our careers. Doing career assessment or self-evaluation, planning our career path, and selecting continuing education offerings are basic steps in coping with these predictable events.

Is Career Assessment Timely?

Evaluating our career status and progress becomes timely in a variety of situations. On the preventive and positive side, selecting appropriate continuing education offerings, considering additional formal studies in academic and institutional settings, and gaining self-knowledge all are legitimate reasons for career assessment. On the remedial or negative side, career assessment helps us face vocational crises, allows us to cope with personal or professional deficiencies, and provides a setting for exploring recurring and troublesome patterns in our ministries.

Essentially, career assessment encourages ministers to search for answers to two questions. (1) What are my strengths and limits for ministry? (2) What's God getting me ready for next? Knowing ourselves and having a sense of God's movement in our lives provide a broad foundation for assessing how we're doing and where we're going in our ministries.

A network of denominational and ecumenical career assessment centers across the nation make evaluative and consultative services available to ministers. Other written materials and local counseling resources undergird ministers' efforts to keep careers alive and growing.

Overview: Career Development for Leaders

Leaders take command of our vocations through the decisions we make. We decide how to expand and deepen our support networks. We identify our career anchors. We face each life stage realistically and prepare for future ones. We evaluate our career progress and decide how we will continue to grow in ministry leadership.

Review Questions

1. Who are some types of career guides and encouragers?
2. Which career anchors mean most to you?
3. Which life and career stage are you in now?
4. How are you planning for your future as a leader in ministry?

Notes

1. Edgar H. Schein, *Career Dynamics* (Reading, Mass.: Addison-Wesley Publishing Co., 1978), pp. 124-72.
2. A full treatment of the distinctives of special leading and natural leading are found in the research bulletin by Frederick R. Kling, *The Motivations of Ministerial Candidates* (Princeton, N.J.: Educational Testing Service, 1959), pp. 11-19.
3. The framework for this section is suggested by Daniel J. Levinson, et al., *The Seasons of a Man's Life* (New York: Alfred A. Knopf, 1978).
4. For information on continuing education for ministers, contact SACEM, 3401 Bound Brook Road, Richmond, VA 23227.

Selected Bibliography on Career Development

Biersdorf, John, ed. *Creating an Intentional Ministry*. Nashville: Abingdon Press, 1976.

Glasse, James D. *Profession: Minister*. Nashville: Abingdon Press, 1968.

Levinson, Daniel J., et al. *The Seasons of a Man's Life*. New York: Alfred A. Knopf, 1978.

McGehee, Fred. *A Career Assessment Manual for Ministers*. Nashville: Convention Press, 1981.

Steward, Charles William. *Person and Profession: Career Development in the Ministry*. Nashville: Abingdon Press, 1974.

Super, Donald. *Psychology of Careers*. New York: Harper & Brothers, 1957.

SCRIPTURE INDEX

SUBJECT INDEX

Printed in the United States
5254